T0286043

Cambridge Elements ☰

Elements in Women in Music
edited by
Rhiannon Mathias
Bangor University

LEOKADIYA KASHPEROVA

Biography, 'Memoirs' and 'Recollections of Anton Rubinstein'

Graham Griffiths
City, University of London

CAMBRIDGE
UNIVERSITY PRESS

Shaftesbury Road, Cambridge CB2 8EA, United Kingdom

One Liberty Plaza, 20th Floor, New York, NY 10006, USA

477 Williamstown Road, Port Melbourne, VIC 3207, Australia

314–321, 3rd Floor, Plot 3, Splendor Forum, Jasola District Centre,
New Delhi – 110025, India

103 Penang Road, #05–06/07, Visioncrest Commercial, Singapore 238467

Cambridge University Press is part of Cambridge University Press & Assessment,
a department of the University of Cambridge.

We share the University's mission to contribute to society through the pursuit of
education, learning and research at the highest international levels of excellence.

www.cambridge.org
Information on this title: www.cambridge.org/9781009097239

DOI: 10.1017/9781009093446

First published 2023

A catalogue record for this publication is available from the British Library.

ISBN 978-1-009-09723-9 Paperback
ISSN 2633-6871 (online)
ISSN 2633-6863 (print)

Additional resources for this publication at [insert URL here].

Leokadiya Kashperova

Biography, 'Memoirs' and 'Recollections of Anton Rubinstein'

Elements in Women in Music

DOI: 10.1017/9781009093446
First published online: January 2023

Author for correspondence:
Dr Graham Griffiths, g.griffiths.kashperova@gmail.com

Abstract: Leokadiya Kashperova (1872–1940) was a Russian composer, concert pianist and Stravinsky's most significant piano teacher. Her Romantic compositions were highly regarded by Rimsky-Korsakov and César Cui, and her playing was admired by Balakirev, whose works she premiered and recorded. In 1907, Kashperova performed her own compositions to critical acclaim in Leipzig, Berlin and London. After the 1917 Revolution, barely a note of her music was heard again. Following Kashperova's death in 1940, even her name, once familiar to concert audiences within Russia and abroad, joined her fine music in historical anonymity and oblivion. This publication is the result of twenty years' research culminating in eight study-visits by the author to St Petersburg, Moscow and the Yaroslavl/Kostroma region. The Biography (Section 1) is the first ever written about this composer. Kashperova's 'Memoirs' (Section 2) and her 'Recollections of Anton Rubinstein' (Section 3) are made available in translation for the first time. Together with a new edition of her compositions (Boosey & Hawkes, London), this Element aims to support the restoration of Kashperova to her rightful place in music history as Russia's foremost female composer of the early twentieth century.

This Element also has a video abstract: https://youtu.be/6WQ_BswMUC4

Keywords: Russia, female composer, pianist, Anton Rubinstein, Stravinsky

ISBNs: 9781009097239 (PB), 9781009093446 (OC)
ISSNs: 2633-6871 (online), 2633-6863 (print)

Contents

1 Biography: A Life in Music
Graham Griffiths

**

She was well known in St Petersburg, and Rimsky had praised her
though her name would not appear in Grove *or* Riemann.
I think she might have been listed in a Russian dictionary of the time.

Igor Stravinsky[1]

You want to know whence came the stars above us?
Oh, my child!
The wisest men on earth have tried in vain
To solve the mystery of the stars.

From *Where Do The Stars Come From?*[2]

Leokadiya Aleksandrovna Kashperova (1872–1940) – the stress is on the second syllable, KashPERova[3] – was a Russian concert pianist, composer and piano teacher (see Figure 1). She also possessed a poetic gift, writing the Romantic lyrics to several of her own songs in both Russian and German. As a pianist, she performed regularly in St Petersburg and Moscow, making one foreign tour in 1907; her creativity spanned over fifty years (see Catalogue of Compositions). She was a dedicated teacher in the Russian tradition of combining performance with a full timetable of piano teaching, counting amongst her more celebrated pupils Igor Stravinsky and Alexander Tcherepnin. In later years, she would set down her memoirs (see Section 2) and write a study of her great teacher, Anton Rubinstein (see Section 3). In 1912, the *Russian Musical Gazette* reviewed a 'Clavierabend' presented by Kashperova, describing her as 'a most welcome phenomenon of St Petersburg's musical life'.[4] The programme included the premiere of two major compositions: a Piano Trio in A Minor (which Kashperova considered to be her finest work) for the unusual combination of viola, cello and piano; and *Hommage aux œuvres de Pietro Canonica*, a tribute to the Italian sculptor in seven movements. It was her largest composition for solo piano. Both works were enthusiastically reviewed. Both were subsequently lost amidst the upheavals of the 1917 Revolution and the composer's hurried flight from Petrograd. So, too, was her four-movement

---

[1] Igor Stravinsky and Robert Craft, *Memories and Commentaries* (London: Faber & Faber, 2002), p. 34.

[2] *Where Do the Stars Come From?* (1902). Legend for soprano, baritone, SSAA and pf. Lyrics: Yakov Polonsky. Music: L. A. Kashperova. (All translations in the Biography are by the author unless otherwise stated.)

[3] KashperOVA should be avoided. KASHperova is an alternative, particularly in the masculine form: KASHperov.

[4] *Russkaya Muzikal'naya Gazyeta* [*Russian Musical Gazette*], no. 16 (15 April 1912): Khronika [Chronicle], sections 393–4.

Figure 1 Leokadiya A. Kashperova ca. 1900 around the time she premiered her Piano Concerto op. 2 in Moscow and St Petersburg, and was teaching Igor Stravinsky.[5]

Image: *courtesy of the Russian National Museum of Music, with thanks to Mikhail Bryzgalov and Olga Kuzina.*

Sonata no. 3 in F for cello and piano. Such were the disruptions, it appears that after 1916 hardly a note of Kashperova's music was performed again, not in Imperial Russia nor in the USSR. Following her death in 1940, even her name, once so familiar, joined her fine music in historical anonymity and oblivion.

My research into Kashperova began in 2002 at the University of Bristol, where I explored the impact of her teaching upon Stravinsky's emergence as a concert pianist in the early 1920s.[6] By the time my thesis was completed at Oxford in 2008,

---

[5] Figures 1–4 (using numbers) appear in this Biography. Figures A, AA, and so on (using letters) are available online: www.cambridge.org/Graham_Online appendix.

[6] See Graham Griffiths, 'Leokadiya Kashperova and Stravinsky: The Making of a Concert Pianist', in Graham Griffiths (ed.), *Stravinsky in Context* (Cambridge: Cambridge University Press, 2021), pp. 24–33.

I had placed Stravinsky's absorption with pianism's constructive processes at the centre of his creative re-invention as a neoclassicist – now viewed from the perspective of his relationship with the piano. My subsequent monograph tested this premise against Stravinsky's whole output: eighty-five compositions are considered.[7] The book's analytical focus derived, in embryo, from Stravinsky's undoubtedly transformational experience between 1899 and 1901 as a student of Kashperova, whom he describes in his autobiography as 'this excellent musician'.[8]

Little did I expect the next phase of my research to reveal that 'Stravinsky's piano teacher' was also, indeed primarily, a talented and very successful composer. In my first visit to St Petersburg in April 2014, I was able to locate some of her scores that had lain undisturbed for over a century in the city's libraries and archives. The most important of these early discoveries was her Symphony in B Minor, which had been performed in 1905 in Moscow and St Petersburg, later in Berlin.[9] In 2016 came an important break-through: an archive of materials was located at the Glinka State Consortium of Musical Culture, leading to the editing and restoration of other scores, some from manuscript.[10] Since then, research into Kashperova's biography has continued apace and, thanks to the generous support of other researchers in the United Kingdom, Germany and Russia (see Acknowledgements), it is now possible to publish this short biography, together with Kashperova's writings, in this single Element. Thus another significant landmark has been reached in the restoration of Kashperova to her rightful place in music history: as Russia's foremost woman composer of the early twentieth century – composition representing but one of her many talents.

Leokadiya Aleksandrovna Kashperova – or as she is referred to in Russian and Soviet encyclopaedias Кашперова Леокадия (Александровна) – was born on 4 May Old Style (16 May New Style) 1872 in Lyubim, a village in the Yaroslavl district, 300 km north-east of Moscow.[11] She died on 3 December 1940 in Moscow,

---

[7] Graham Griffiths, *Stravinsky's Piano: Genesis of a Musical Language* (Cambridge: Cambridge University Press, 2013).

[8] Igor Stravinsky, *An Autobiography (1903–1934)* (London: Marion Boyars, 1990), p. 13.

[9] As a consequence of this discovery, the Symphony would also be performed in London – by the BBC Concert Orchestra under Jane Glover, and broadcast on BBC Radio 3 – on International Women's Day (8 March) 2018. See also the final page of the Acknowledgements.

[10] From this material, the Kashperova Edition was created by Boosey & Hawkes (London) with the full authorization of the (re-named) Russian National Museum of Music, Moscow: www.boosey .com/composer/Leokadiya+Kashperova.

[11] Central State Historical Archive of St Petersburg: Archive 361/Inventory 3/File 3051. Amid several crossings-out it appears that 6 May is eventually preferred over 4 May although a more reliable source has '4/16 May 1872': L. A. Kashperova, Воспоминания [*Memoirs*], ed. N. G. Fesenkova, in Музыкальное наследство [*Musical Legacy*], vol. 2, pt 2 (Moscow: Muzyka, 1968), p. 135. Fesenkova would have conferred with Alexei Kashperov with whom she compiled the Kashperova archive (no. 345) at the Russian National Museum of Music, Moscow.

though, at the time of going to press, it has not been possible to confirm the location of her grave. In official documents her first name is given as Elikonida; for example in her two St Petersburg Conservatoire diplomas (1893, 1895)[12] and in her Passport for Life (1898).[13] Following her marriage in 1916 to Sergei Andropov, she performed under the name of Leokadiya Kashperova-Andropova. She was a relative of the Moscow-based pianist and composer Elizaveta (Vladimirovna) Kashperova (1871–1945), a piano teacher at the Moscow Conservatoire between 1921 and 1931. She was therefore also related to the opera composer, Elizaveta's father, Vladimir (Nikitich) Kashperov (1826–94), a professor at the Moscow Conservatoire between 1866 and 1872. Vladimir Kashperov had enjoyed considerable success in Italy with productions of his operas *Maria Tudor* (Milan), *Rienzi* (Florence) and *Consuelo* (Venice) staged between 1859 and 1865. He attended Glinka's funeral in Paris in 1857. Later, in Moscow, he was a close associate of Tchaikovsky, Nikolai Rubinstein, Herzen, Ogarëv and Turgenev, and set librettos to works by Ostrovsky (*The Storm*, 1867) and Gogol (*Taras Bulba*, 1893).[14]

Leokadiya's unusual, un-Russian 'official' name, Elikonida, was surely the result of the tradition, prevalent in rural Russia where she was born, of leaving the responsibility of naming a new arrival to the Orthodox priest who officiates at the child's baptism. As Kashperova was born on 4/16 May her christening would have fallen close to 28 May, the saint's day for St Elikonida of Thessaloniki.

Kashperova's father, Aleksandr Vladimirovich Kashperov (1838–98), had studied law at the Demidov Lyceum in Yaroslavl. Documents held in the archive of the regional assembly in nearby Kostroma – the stress is on the last syllable, KostroMA – reveal that he was subsequently enlisted for military service and was decorated with a bronze medal for his participation in the 'pacification of the mutiny in the Kingdom of Poland', referred to nowadays as the January Uprising, of 1863–4.[15] The following year, Lieutenant Kashperov returned home to take up his first post, as a judge in the rural district of Lyubim from 1866. He was subsequently elected to the Honorable Justices of Bui County in 1878 and re-elected in 1884. The family was descended from the noble line of 'Kashpirovs' whose roots can be traced to the eighteenth century. By the time of Leokadiya Kashperova's birth in 1872, the family regularly wintered in

---

[12] Central State Historical Archive of St Petersburg: Archive 7/Inventory 2/File 1793.

[13] Issued on 30 July 1898. Central State Historical Archive of St Petersburg: Archive 361/Inventory 3/File 3051.

[14] Olga Kuzina, 'Неизвестные автографы П. И. Чайковского в архиве В. Ф. Одоевского' [Unknown Tchaikovsky Manuscripts in the Odoyevsky Archive] in *Almanac*, no. 2, ed. M. P. Rakhmanova (Moscow: Glinka State Consortium of Musical Culture, 2003), pp. 298–306 (p. 300).

[15] Information researched by local historians Larisa Pukhacheva (Kostroma) and Irina Ivanovna Zenkina (Yaroslavl), July 2019 in the Kostroma Region Historical Archives (scans 2800–40).

Kostroma, spending the summer months in their architecturally splendid mansion at Bochatino, which had been built around 1830 and modelled on the fashionable English Regency style (See Figure A).[16] The estate extended to over 400 acres. In her memoirs, Kashperova acknowledges her upbringing within the 'landed gentry', giving this as the reason for the breadth and intensity of her early tutoring, particularly in foreign languages and the creative arts.

Her mother, Maria Aleksandrovna (1849–1929), performed a significant role in guiding her family's musical and cultural education.[17] She played the piano, painted and also wrote poetry, providing the lyrics for Kashperova's eight *Children's Tales in Song* (1907). Leokadiya was one of four children, three girls and an older brother; she would later compose a piano suite *In the Midst of Nature* (1910) for her younger sister Elizaveta. Kashperova learned the piano from the age of four, initially from her mother, then with Zinaida (Fedorovna) Khomutova, who at one time had studied with Katerina (Kristoforovna) Rubinstein, the mother of the two celebrated Rubinstein brothers, Anton and Nikolai, founders of the St Petersburg and Moscow Conservatoires. From the age of six, Kashperova had lessons from Maria (Fedorovna) Fiuson, who introduced to her young pupil the music of Mozart and Beethoven by reading through many of their symphonies at the piano, in duet arrangement.

Kashperova's upbringing had been immersed in literature. At a tender age she was already copying out poems, prayers and psalms in German and English, often intended as affectionate Mother's Day offerings: 'She sets me on her knee / Very often, for some kisses / Oh! How good I'll try to be / For such a dear Mamma as this is' being a typical example, written when she was barely seven.[18] Life in the remote countryside was enlivened by theatrical performances in the music room ('with white columns'), Kashperova and her sisters writing the plays themselves. There, the narrative of Polonsky's dramatic ballad *The Eagle and the Snake*, which she would later choose as a song lyric, might well have first come to her attention, being ideal for enactment via informal, improvised representation.[19]

---

[16] Bochatino was designed by the same architect, N. I. Mitkin, as a prominent mansion built a few years earlier in the centre of Kostroma. This would become the London Hotel, so-named for its architectural style and, from 1857, the provincial court-house. Figure A, see: www.cambridge .org/Graham_Online appendix.

[17] From the age of seven, Kashperova was learning English and German under her mother's guidance. Documents held at the Russian National Museum of Music (Moscow) reveal that between 1879 and 1881 Kashperova enjoyed copying out favourite texts – for instance, a prayer in German ('Hilf', Herr Jesu'), a psalm in English ('Psalm XXIII') and poetry ('To my dear Mamma', 'Time flies', 'Flowers', 'Thanks'). These were all addressed to her mother and written in neat calligraphy: Archive 345/104–112.

[18] Archive 345/108.

[19] Yakov Polonsky (1819–98) was highly regarded in his day for maintaining the lyrical tradition of Russian Romantic poetry, especially that of its greatest figure, Alexander Pushkin (1799–1837).

In 1883, at the age of eleven, she was enrolled at the music academy in Moscow directed by Nadezhda Muromtseva, a former pupil of Nikolai Rubinstein at the Moscow Conservatoire. There, she began to perform piano solos in public whilst acquiring a passion for chamber music and for the music of Beethoven. In her memoirs, she recalls attending Anton Rubinstein's performance of Sonata op. 109 and how the beauty of the theme in the 'Theme and Variations' finale had woken her up during the night to hear 'an authentic human voice penetrate my soul. This voice brought me to tears.'

By 1888, Kashperova, now aged sixteen, was established in St Petersburg in an apartment close to the Conservatoire, at Ofitserskaya ulitsa, no. 26 apt. 30. (The street was later renamed Rimsky-Korsakov Prospekt.)[20] The Central State Historical Archive of St Petersburg holds a letter (2 August 1888) signed by Kashperova's mother addressed to the Conservatoire's admissions office. She requests that her daughter be admitted to attend 'courses in piano, theory of composition and other academic subjects as an external student'.[21] At the second attempt she was granted a place, studying at the St Petersburg Conservatoire for a total of seven years, from 1888 to 1895 (See Figure AA).[22] In 1893, the year she graduated from Rubinstein's Special Piano class, she was awarded the Schröder Pianoforte Prize.[23] In 1895, she graduated for a second time, from Nikolai Solovyov's theory and composition class. At her graduation concert, even though Rubinstein had been vehemently opposed to women conductors ('just a farcical idea'; see Section 3), Kashperova directed soloists, chorus and orchestra in her own composition *Orvasi* (1895), a cantata with texts by the Symbolist poet Dmitri Merezhkovsky (1866–1941).[24]

His poetry was set by a wide range of prominent Russian composers in the nineteenth and twentieth centuries.

[20] In 1892 she was living at 2 Yamskaya Street, Apartment 15. In December 1896 César Cui wrote to her at 1 Dmitrovsky Pereulok [Lane] which is located close to Dostoevsky's former residence, now the 'F. M. Dostoevsky Literary-Memorial Museum'.

[21] Central State Historical Archive of St Petersburg: Archive 361/Inventory 3/File 3051. The address given on this letter is: Kostromskaya guberniya [region], Buiski uezd [parish], Bochatino mansion, on the river Volga. Written in the margin of this letter is a note in Kashperova's hand (signed and dated 30 May 1898) indicating that the Conservatoire had returned all her personal documents. The archive also holds an earlier letter from Kashperova to the Conservatoire (dated 20 March 1893); it demonstrates that as an external student she is obliged formally to request permission from the Conservatoire director to be allowed to sit the exam for 'Special Piano' as a pupil of Anton Rubinstein.

[22] Figure AA see: www.cambridge.org/Graham_Online appendix

[23] A prize awarded annually by the St Petersburg-based piano manufacturers C. M. Schröder (1818–1917).

[24] Ludmila Korabelnikova, *Alexander Tcherepnin: The Saga of a Russian Emigré Composer* (Bloomington: Indiana University Press, 2008), p. 6.

The four years she spent in the Special Piano class of Anton Rubinstein, that towering figure of Russian music, are generously documented by Kashperova (see Section 3). As for her experience of studying with Solovyov, one must rely upon a single witness statement from fellow student Samuel Maikapar (1867–1938), whose canon of children's piano works is still held in high regard. Solovyov, famed to this day for his comic squib, surely intentionally so (namely, that Tchaikovsky's Piano Concerto no. 1 'like the first pancake, is a flop'),[25] was evidently fond of the *bon mot*. His teaching style probably reflected as much, to the distaste of Kashperova who, daily, would have compared his lightness with the gravitas of the great and (since his death in 1894) immortal Rubinstein. Maikapar reminisces:

> [Kashperova] had spent four years in the piano class of A. G. Rubinstein. Gifted in both [piano and composition] she also stood apart for her serious attitude to study and her extraordinary directness of character. In his lectures Solovyov liked to make jokes, but not always successfully. I remember one occasion, after some particularly unsuccessful witticisms, that displeasure was registered very clearly across Kashperova's face. Noting this, Solovyov enquired: 'Didn't you like that?' 'No, I didn't like it at all!' she replied, frankly. Solovyov wasn't angry with her, but just laughed and continued with his lecture. A few years after graduation she presented me with a printed score of her symphony and its piano transcription in the Bessel edition [St Petersburg's leading music publishers].[26]

The Central State Historical Archive also preserves Kashperova's two diplomas, the first (29 May 1893)[27] recording her graduation from Rubinstein's 'Special Piano' class. This confirms that she 'completed all examined subjects and has shown her abilities in her main subjects: piano performance in the class of the Rector A. G. Rubinstein: *Excellent*. And in secondary subjects: Theory of Music (special class: Fugue) and Encyclopaedia: *Excellent*'. The second diploma (26 May 1895) records Kashperova's graduation from Solovyov's composition class and that, as a consequence of this, she has been awarded the title of Free Artist. The fourteen signatories include Anna Esipova (pianist), Felix Blumenfeld (conductor), F. Czerny (piano teacher and future colleague at the St Petersburg Music School), Anatoly K. Lyadov (1855–1914) and N. A. Rimsky-Korsakov (1844–1908) (see Figure B: www.cambridge.org/Graham_Online appendix)

---

[25] 'Novoye Vremya', St Petersburg, 13 November 1875.
[26] S. M. Maikapar, *The Years of Study and Musical Activity* (Moscow, 1938). This is an excerpt from chapter 4: 'Professor N. F. Solovyov: My Completion of His Course in Compositional Theory'. Available online: www.beethoven.ru/en/node/987 (accessed 7 April 2021). In chapter 2, Maikapar recalls studying 'ensemble' with Leopold Auer.
[27] The text of the diploma has 26 May.

Hardly had the ink dried on her diploma than Kashperova was completing her first major unsupervised composition. As she describes in her memoirs:

> My first independent composition was a sonata for cello and piano. I wrote it in the summer following my graduation from the Conservatoire [1895] and wanted to show it to Aleksandr Verzhbilovich [the cello professor] in the autumn but changed my mind. Later, I timidly admitted that I had written a sonata. After we played the first movement through he exclaimed: 'What a surprising young lady you are! How beautiful it is and how well it suits the cello!' Verzhbilovich showed it to Rimsky-Korsakov and Lyadov who were both pleased with the composition, Lyadov suggesting some changes. But my friends and I did not like these, so I decided to publish it in its original form. I soon wrote a second sonata which Verzhbilovich also played beautifully in St Petersburg and Moscow.[28]

These early cello sonatas, particularly their luxuriant piano parts, mark Kashperova's spectacular entry into St Petersburg's professional concert world as the Conservatoire's prize-winning Rubinstein protegee. Yet, her personal reflections on their composition, despite such enthusiastic reception, reveal an emerging composer who needed the support of her fellow students to resist the interference of (male) authority intent on 'correcting' her music. Lyadov's suggestions were rejected – this, surely, a significant moment of self-assertion.

Kashperova's Cello Sonatas, op. 1, no. 1 in G and no. 2 in E Minor were composed between 1895 and 1896. Both works are in four expansive movements and display such compositional assurance and breadth of expression they must surely rank amongst the most impressive 'opus 1' creations by any young composer. These qualities also define her Piano Concerto in A Minor (1900) and Symphony in B Minor (1905), not least in the memorable passages for solo cello that feature in both works. (Such quirks of orchestration would later invoke Balakirev's displeasure, but they are evidence that Kashperova distanced herself from the Russian nationalist style.) The Cello Sonatas present considerable yet deeply rewarding challenges to the performers, particularly the pianist, for the brilliance of the piano writing gives a clear indication of Kashperova's elevated technique. Both works offer musical audiences today a substantial feast of Russian Romanticism at its most lyrical.

According to a concert review that autumn in one of St Petersburg's German-language newspapers (*Mährisches Tagblatt*, 20 November 1895), Kashperova was singled out, following a recital presented by all the former Rubinstein students, as '*die Allerbegabteste*' ('the most gifted of them all'). Even the

---

[28] Translation: Patricia Cockrell, 2019. See Section 2. Kashperova was the pianist in this cello–piano duo, which would perform regularly until Verzhbilovich's death in 1911.

cello professor was keen to form an artistic partnership with this brilliant young graduate. Aleksandr Verzhbilovich, dedicatee of the Sonatas, was also section leader of the Maryinsky Theatre Orchestra.[29] Together with the distinguished violinist and teacher Leopold Auer, a regular chamber ensemble was formed and, thus, the piano trio became a favourite genre for Kashperova, not least for giving value on several occasions during her career to both her talents as composer and performer. A week after the recital, Kashperova performed Rubinstein's Piano Quartet, op. 66, with Auer, Fyodor Hildebrandt and Verzhbilovich at the Fifth Quartet Meeting of the Russian Musical Society (on 28 November). This momentous year ended on an even higher note, with Kashperova as the soloist in Rubinstein's Piano Concerto no. 5 (op. 94, in E-flat) at the Tenth Symphonic Meeting of the Russian Musical Society under the direction of Max von Erdmansdörfer.[30]

1898

As Kashperova began to establish her career she also indulged her long-standing interest in poetry by becoming personally acquainted with Yakov Polonsky, and often attended his literary gatherings. When the poet died in 1898, Kashperova responded by setting one of his most celebrated ballads, *The Eagle and the Snake*, for the benefit of the memorial fund established to support Polonsky's widow and family.[31] Kashperova's setting, for baritone and piano, displays her intuitive sense of drama and atmosphere, qualities that had become intrinsic to all her compositions. No evidence survives of a public rendition of this dramatic 'ballad' although, given the circumstances, it was surely performed privately on numerous occasions, especially at 'Les Vendredis Polonsky'. As Kashperova mentions in her memoirs, she herself regularly hosted 'musical evenings at home on Tuesdays'. It is therefore highly likely that in this domestic context she would have programmed *The Eagle and the Snake* (1902) alongside renditions of her *Songs of Love: 12 Romances* (1904) long before these were published.

1899

Within a few years, Kashperova had become a regular feature of the city's musical calendar, frequently performing in the most august company. On 15 March 1899, César Cui (1835–1918) wrote to Balakirev inviting him to attend

---

[29] Among Verzhbilovich's pupils would be Leopold, b.1892, father of Mstislav Rostropovich, 1927–2007.
[30] Erdmansdörfer may have demonstrated empathy with Kashperova's creativity: he was married to the Austrian pianist-composer Pauline Fichtner (1847–1916).
[31] Polonsky's daughter Natalia would later marry Stravinsky's cousin Nikolai Yelachich.

an informal demonstration of arias from his new opera *Saracen* (1898) 'tomor-row, Wednesday, at 8 p.m.'.[32] Among the guests would be the most respected music critic of the time, Vladimir Stasov; also Ilya Repin, the famous portrait painter. Cui signs off his invitation with 'Kashperova accompanies, I sing'. No first name or further explanation was required.

In 1899, Kashperova was invited by Fyodor Stravinsky, principal baritone at the Maryinsky Opera House, to give regular piano lessons to his son, Igor (see Figure BB: www.cambridge.org/Graham_online appendix).[33] Fyodor might have been prompted to extend this invitation to Kashperova having seen her or, possibly, conversed with her at Polonsky's funeral, which they had both attended the previous November; the celebrated Pushkinist poet had died on 30 October 1898. Around the same time, Kashperova began composing her Piano Concerto in A Minor, op. 2, completing it in 1900. She premiered this work, her first major orchestral score, on 17 January 1901 in Moscow under the direction of Vasily Safonov – later, principal conductor of the New York Philharmonic from 1906 until Gustav Mahler's appointment in 1909. The concerto was performed again on 3 February in St Petersburg under the direction of Max Fiedler (who later conducted the Boston Symphony Orchestra from 1908 to 1912). These experiences brought Kashperova wider recognition and inaugurated a decade of increasingly ambitious and prestigious engagements and commissions.

The orchestral colours that Kashperova employs in her Piano Concerto are often achieved by allocating generous solos to the wind and brass, this sonority becoming a characteristic of her preferred orchestral palette. Noteworthy, too, are unexpected glimpses of chamber music, in the last movement for example, when the piano combines fleetingly with solo violin and solo cello in passages that illustrate the composer's declared fondness for the piano trio genre, and might possibly have been written with her professional colleagues in mind. The concerto's quick outer movements (*Molto allegro* and *Allegro con anima*) admirably portray the vivacious personality of their composer, recalled by Monika Hunnius as offering those around her 'an abundance of joy, excitement and fun … She never ceases to surprise us all!'[34] The central movement, by contrast, is a tender *Andante* which offers the listener a gem of musical poetry.

---

[32] César A. Cui, *Избранные письма* [*Selected Letters*], ed. I. L. Gusin (Leningrad: State Music Publishers, 1955), letter 272, p. 199.

[33] The first of many entries in Fyodor Stravinsky's account books that mention Kashperova appears on 12 [24] January 1900. See the top line: 'To the piano teacher L. A. Kashperova. 5 lessons given to Igor since 1 December 1899 – 25 roubles'. (Fyodor S. Akimenko was later paid 6 roubles for four lessons on the theory of music.) Image courtesy of the F. I. Stravinsky Family Fund (Moscow & Venice).

[34] Monika Hunnius, *Mein Weg zur Kunst* [*My Path to Art*] (Hamburg: Verlag tradition-GmbH, 1925), p. 252; see also pp. 253–7. (Hunnius was related to the author Hermann Hesse.)

There is no record of Stravinsky attending a performance of Kashperova's music, although she might well have demonstrated passages of the Piano Concerto to him. It is likely, even, that she shared with the whole Stravinsky family the exciting news of her debut in Moscow, as the soloist in her own composition. Certainly, it is interesting to observe that two decades later when Stravinsky launched himself onto the international stage as a pianist he chose a familiar, if not identical, route: by composing his *own* piano concerto – the *Concerto for Piano and Wind Instruments* (1923–4) – which he *himself* premiered, Koussevitsky conducting. Admittedly, in Paris in 1923 Stravinsky is unlikely to have recalled his former piano teacher. Rather, he was motivated by his own drive towards neoclassicism, if not also sensing a degree of artistic rivalry with Prokofiev, whose third piano concerto had received a performance in Paris under Koussevitsky's baton the previous year. Nevertheless, both Kashperova's and Stravinsky's piano concertos led to a new and exciting phase in their composers' professional trajectories. There are no stylistic similarities, of course, between Kashperova's Romantic warmth and Stravinsky's icy objectivity. However, in terms of piano-writing (or, as Rimsky-Korsakov called it, 'keyboard instrumentation') there is, I believe, a curious if unconscious commonality: the creative drive of both composers to generate virtuosity is often channelled, coincidence or not, into the pianist's *left* hand, which is required to negotiate widely spaced 'extreme' arpeggios – awkwardly angular when expressive and *andante*, fiendishly technical when *molto allegro*.

Stravinsky studied with Kashperova from 1899 to 1902.[35] In *Chroniques de ma vie* ('An Autobiography', 1936) he reluctantly gives her due credit: 'I must say that, notwithstanding our differences of opinion, this excellent musician managed to give a new impetus to my piano-playing and to the development of my technique.'[36] However, by 1960 she is referred to by Stravinsky in a more caustic tone, as 'an excellent pianist and a blockhead – a not unusual combination. By which I mean that her aesthetics and her bad taste were impregnable, but her pianism was of a high order.'[37] Regrettably, it is from such commentaries that Western opinion of Kashperova has been formed thus far. Stephen Walsh offers his conciliatory insight: 'The image of rebellion suited the ageing Stravinsky who wanted to distance himself from the narrow rules and petty preoccupations of provincial St Petersburg and from the insecure young man who accepted this village green as if it were the

---

[35] For further discussion of Stravinsky as a piano student of Kashperova, see Griffiths, *Stravinsky in Context*, chapter 3; see also Griffiths, *Stravinsky's Piano*.

[36] Stravinsky, *An Autobiography*, p. 13.

[37] Stravinsky and Craft, *Memories and Commentaries*, pp. 33–4.

whole planet. He wanted, rather, to be thought of as a free spirit, a phenomenon without a history.'[38] Without doubt, it is largely due to this 'history' –
that is, the excellent technique and sense of *métier* that Kashperova commu-
nicated to Stravinsky at this time – that he was able, twenty-two years later, to
transform himself into a concert pianist; and, after a mere eight months'
preparation, make his professional debut in May 1924 in the premiere of the
Concerto for Piano and Wind Instruments on the stage of the Paris Opéra
under Serge Koussevitzky.

Stravinsky's other references to Kashperova are scarcely less hostile: 'I had
to battle with my second piano mistress, a pupil and admirer of Anton
Rubinstein … completely obsessed by her adoration of her illustrious master,
whose views she blindly accepted.'[39] True enough, two-thirds of her memoirs
(1929) will be given over to a portrait of the enigmatic *persona* of Rubinstein,
whilst also offering a precious and detailed insight into his teaching methods.[40]
According to Stravinsky's *own* testimony, he was the beneficiary of her at times
quite unorthodox teaching. She was a composer after all, therefore interested in
contemporary musical trends. Having criticised her 'narrowness and formulae'
in the following terms – 'I had great difficulty in making her accept the scores of
… Rimsky-Korsakov' – Stravinsky then invalidates this criticism by revealing:
'We played Rimsky's operas together four-hands and I remember deriving
pleasure from *Noch pered Rozhdestvom* (*Christmas Eve*) this way.'[41]
Rimsky's opera had been premiered as recently as December 1895. By reading
through this work with Stravinsky at the piano Kashperova evidenced neither
disinterest in Rimsky-Korsakov's scores nor narrowness in her pedagogic
methods. One wonders how many piano teachers before or since would intro-
duce their pupils to the latest in contemporary opera?

Kashperova's exploration of piano technique and piano teaching, as observed
through the prism of her 'Recollections of Anton Rubinstein', reveals that she was
appreciative of a much wider range of methodologies and performance practices
than Stravinsky would have us believe. She recommends, for example, that
students should study the greatest pianists past and present (i.e. not only
Rubinstein) particularly when launching their career, at that precise moment
when they may still be uncertain about their own direction: 'Young people are
often not confident enough to stand on their own two feet, to work independently.

---

[38] Stephen Walsh, *Stravinsky: A Creative Spring: Russia and France 1882–1934* (London: Pimlico, 2002), p. 53.

[39] Stravinsky, *An Autobiography*, pp. 12–13.

[40] Kashperova's observations provide a fascinating departure from today's 'received', though often misleading, view of Rubinstein (see Section 3).

[41] Stravinsky and Craft, *Memories and Commentaries*, p. 25.

That is the time for them to listen attentively to the great virtuosi and to learn from their methods in order to gain support for their own individual work.'[42]

Stravinsky comments further that 'Mlle Kashperova's only idiosyncrasy as a teacher was in forbidding me all use of the pedals. I had to sustain with my fingers, like an organist – an omen, perhaps, as I have never been a pedal composer.'[43] Such a dry, 'Baroque' texture was intrinsic to the sonority of Stravinsky's neoclassical works for piano solo, particularly the *Sonate pour piano* (1924) and the *Sérénade en la* (1925). Under Kashperova's direction Stravinsky's progress was rapid; and fundamental to this new impetus was a new professional attitude. She can be credited with encouraging Stravinsky to put aside the frivolous anarchy of improvisation for which he had an undoubted facility. Under her firm guidance, for the first time in his life, he embraced serious piano study. Furthermore, as his correspondence with his parents at the time suggests, he was keenly motivated by such self-discipline.[44] It appears that from the moment he began lessons with Kashperova he no longer played the piano merely for the entertainment of others. At the age of eighteen, he now took satisfaction in engaging fully with the development or, to use a neoclassical term, the 'construction' of his own technique, marking a significant indication of his emerging musical maturity in this notoriously late developer. Under Kashperova's influence, 'playing the piano' now signified dedication to the improvement of his technique according to *pal'tserazvitel'nykh zanyatii* [finger development exercises] – at least, Stravinsky respected the need for them.[45] Kashperova not only taught him how to acquire an advanced piano technique, she also modelled the mental discipline of practising the long hours necessary to maintain it. One may surmise that, armed with this experience, Stravinsky was able to prepare for his professional debut as a concert pianist two decades later. Whether he recognised it at the time is debatable, but Kashperova was an excellent role model for the young Stravinsky. She was a composer-pianist, after all, and a successful representative of this demanding double-profession to which the mature Stravinsky would one day aspire.

1902

On 31 March 1902, Kashperova gave the first performance of Aleksandr Glazunov's Second Piano Sonata (no. 2 in E, op. 75). Ludmila Korabelnikova

[42] Kashperova, *Vospominaniya*, p. 150. Translation: Roger Cockrell (see Section 3).
[43] Stravinsky and Craft, *Memories & Commentaries*, pp. 25–6.
[44] Letter dated 23 August 1900; in Viktor Varunts, *I. F. Stravinskiy: Perepiska s russkimi korrespondentami. Materialï k biographi*, vol. 1. (Moscow: Sovyetskiy Kompozitor, 1988 [1977]), p. 88; see also Graham Griffiths, *Stravinsky's Piano*, pp. 109–11.
[45] For more information on the significance of this process, see Griffiths, *Stravinsky's Piano*. Concerning the notion of 'pal'tserazvitiye', see especially pp. 109–11.

writes that 'the press praised her world premiere performance of [this work] at one of the "Evenings of Modern Music"'.[46] A significant new professional relationship was thus established. Three years later one of the first congratulatory gifts that Glazunov received upon his appointment as director of the Conservatoire in 1905 was a signed copy of Kashperova's Symphony in B Minor, marking a decade since her graduation (see Figure 7 in the Acknowledgements, p.71).

The year 1902 also saw the publication of Kashperova's second Polonsky setting, *In Reply to a Child's Question: Where Do The Stars Come From?*, a 'legend' for soprano, baritone, SSAA chorus and piano.[47] This delightful work illustrates Kashperova's attraction to themes of childhood, even of an idealised child's world of innocence and reassuring familial love, combining nostalgia, domesticity, mysticism and enchanting poetic fantasy. The front cover of the Bessel first edition displays a charming and refined illustration featuring the narrative's main players: a starry night-sky, a field of (sad) flowers and, centre-stage, a small child clearly enthralled at the magic of it all.

1904

Kashperova's twelve *Songs of Love: 12 Romances* were published in 1904 as two sets of six, subtitled *Dreams* and *Reality*. No evidence has yet been recovered of any public performance in Kashperova's lifetime, not even by the work's dedicatee, soprano Anna Zherebtsova. However, it is known that Kashperova sang them at her regular musical Tuesdays. Indeed, the transparency of the piano writing strongly suggests that she would accompany *herself*, at the piano, and would have been very comfortable doing so for she was passionate about singing.

Kashperova was also responsible for the lyrics of *Songs of Love*, which may well have emerged from her own bittersweet experiences of life and love; she was not to marry until 1916 at the age of forty-four.[48] That the lyrics of *Songs of Love* might express personal sentiments is a view supported by Hunnius's account of a summer school that Kashperova attended two years later at an Estonian resort. Finding herself far from St Petersburg and in relaxed holiday mood, one evening Kashperova opens up to her fellow students: 'Suddenly she tells us of the love of her life, illustrating her story with songs appropriate to her

---

[46] Korabelnikova, *Alexander Tcherepnin*, p. 6.

[47] In the Kashperova Edition (Boosey & Hawkes), the title is abbreviated to *Where Do the Stars Come From?*

[48] While other female pianists graduating with her – musicians she greatly admired (e.g. Sophie Yakimovskaya) – married early to raise a young family, Kashperova remained single and pursued a full-time career. Sofia Poznanskaya, another member of Rubinstein's Special Piano class, also married early, later relocating to Warsaw where she maintained a high-profile career as a concert pianist and teacher.

narrative.' Could these have been the *Songs of Love*? Hunnius is clearly moved by what she hears and sees: 'We observe this wonderful, yet unfamiliar world, full of intensely singular experiences. In the twilight, the sea has become quite still. Only Lyolya's eyes are gleaming. Over the water her voice carries, high, sweet and emotive.'[49]

While steadily adding to her ever-growing portfolio of compositions during the winter seasons, in the summer holidays Aunt Lyolya (Тётя Лёля: 'Tyotya Lyolya') would return to idyllic Bochatino where she would 'throw [herself] headlong into the family lives of [her] sisters in all their joys and sorrows'.

On 16 December 1904, Kashperova gave the first performance of her Piano Trio in D Major, op. 3, with B. S. Kamensky and S. E. Butkevich in the prestigious Meklenburg-Strelitski chamber music series.

1905

The Symphony in B Minor, premiered and published in 1905, is Kashperova's grandest composition. Such is its expressive range, technical assurance and melodic appeal one can only regret that she never found the opportunity to write again for large instrumental forces. It is testimony to Kashperova's originality that the Symphony betrays her sympathies not only for the Russian symphonic tradition but also for the central European tradition. Indeed, upon hearing the work broadcast on BBC Radio 3 in March 2018, a personal acquaintance of the author likened the experience to a river journey, not on the Volga, but on the Rhine or the Danube. True, the Scherzo and the prelude to the final movement offer melodies that are indicated in the score as '*Thème russe*' yet these surely betray the composer's interest in creating her *own* 'folk music' in the Russian style, much as Dvořák did on several occasions with those 'Bohemian' themes which he himself devised.

Perhaps the most impressive aspect of Kashperova's Symphony is the polish of its instrumental writing. That this concert pianist should write for strings, for example, with such competence will not surprise anyone already familiar with Kashperova's early cello sonatas or posthumous piano trio. In the Symphony her instinct for instrumental timbre extends to every section of the orchestra. The work abounds in felicitous solos for woodwinds, horns and brass with beautiful examples; also (as in the Piano Concerto) there are solos for violin and cello, once again reflecting her well-established friendship with, and respect for, her chamber music colleagues, especially Leopold Auer and Aleksandr Verzhbilovich.

Furthermore, Kashperova's score reveals some effective and original ensemble-writing within the orchestral texture: the first movement's cello solo to the accompaniment of a quartet of French horns is a memorable example.

---

[49] Hunnius, *Mein Weg zur Kunst*, pp. 252–4. Lyolya is the diminutive form of Leokadiya.

Such subtleties mark out Kashperova as a composer of individuality. Not content
to follow the example of the older generation of Russian Nationalists, she
contributed her personal voice to the established reputation of Russian composers
not least through her imaginative orchestration. Equally notable is Kashperova's
exploitation of the extremes of register, which is also a characteristic of the piano
writing in her chamber music and art-songs. In the slow introduction to the
Symphony the violins soar to unexpected heights whilst the *Andante*'s closing
bars plunge ever deeper, possibly reflecting the impact of the final bars of
Tchaikovsky's *Pathétique* and the last breath of its composer who, one recalls,
died just nine days after that work's premiere in 1893. Yet, Kashperova's uplifting
Finale (*Molto allegro*) emphatically does not follow this solemn script. On the
contrary, the modest 'Russian theme' (*Andante sostenuto*) on cor anglais, which
heralds the journey to the musical summit, is transformed in the closing bars into
triumphant life-assertion. The whole orchestra, as it were, lights up the vast sky of
the Russian hinterland in a sustained and iridescent sunrise of blazing colour and
majesty. There is no sub-title or nickname to this symphony but, upon hearing it, a
torrent of descriptive labels may spring to mind, each one more appropriate than
the last at reflecting Kashperova's pæan not only to Russian nature but also, by
association, to the *russkaya dusha* (русская душа); that is, to the Russian soul.[50]

1906

Kashperova maintained the highest regard for singers and singing. As mentioned, in 1906 she attended a course at the resort of Neuhäuser near
Königsberg.[51] Her intention was 'to learn from the artistry', as she put it, of
Raimond von Zur-Mühlen (1854–1931).[52] Kashperova would have known of
this celebrated tenor by reputation: he had been chosen by Rubinstein for the
title role in his 'sacred opera' *Christus* and performed this at the composer's
final public engagements as conductor, in Berlin and Stuttgart in the summer of
1894. Zur-Mühlen was widely credited with developing the *Lieder-Abend* as a
recital formula, having often performed with Clara Schumann; Brahms had
claimed him his 'ideal interpreter'. His annual masterclasses on the Baltic coast
were attended by singers from all over Europe, even Japan and India. The course
administrator, Monika Hunnius, would recall in her memoirs that Kashperova,

---

[50] See also Rowan Williams, 'The Russian Soul' in Griffiths, *Stravinsky in Context*, pp. 50–7.
[51] Renamed Kaliningrad in 1945.
[52] Zur-Mühlen (1854-1931) retired from the concert stage at the age of fifty to dedicate himself to
       teaching. He moved to England, first to London, later offering residential courses at Wiston Old
       Rectory, near Steyning (West Sussex). There, amongst his many international students, he taught
       the American bass baritone Paul Robeson. (Information provided by West Sussex Record Office
       and Steyning Museum.)

soon after her arrival, declared to everyone's surprise (after all, by that time, she already enjoyed a considerable reputation as a concert-pianist and composer): 'Let me be one of *you* … Singing is the most beautiful art of all!'

> One evening [Hunnius writes] we were all sitting on the beach watching the sun go down, the waves gently lapping the shore. Lyolya inclines her head backwards, resting her hands loosely on her lap.
>
> She observes neither the sea nor any of us around her. She is picturing the remote countryside of her Russian homeland, breathing the air of the birch-forests and the freshly-mown hay, hearing familiar Russian folksongs fill the tranquil summer evening. She begins to sing in her sweet, clear, and characterful voice.
>
> Her songs awaken in us, too, a longing for meadows and fields after the summer sun has gone down and for such total and peaceful isolation.[53]

If this episode reveals Kashperova's intimate, poetic, very Russian spirit – and also, indeed, the captivating spell she cast on those around her – then the following anecdote suggests that she possessed a big personality and an endearing, somewhat eccentric *joie de vivre*. The singing course drew to a close and, after much singing and dancing, as Hunnius relates:

> We all hastened for home, to the four corners of the globe. I decided to travel to Berlin to spend another eight days with some of my compatriots. Lyolya Kashperova wanted to travel on her own, directly back to her homeland.
>
> So, there we were, in our lodgings in Berlin, seated at the window. It was a rainy and dismal Autumn afternoon. A droshky cab pulls up and who gets out, but Lyolya! We rush down to the street to greet her. 'Lyolya, didn't you want to go straight home?!' Her eyes sparkle like two beaming suns. She grasps our hands: 'But how wonderful it is to be together again!' she says. 'It was so miserable, travelling alone, so I decided to catch up with you all. Let's make the journey to the Russian border together!'
>
> We bring her upstairs to our room amidst much hilarity and joy. 'Oh, Lyolya, you are just like a child! No-one makes a detour from Königsberg to Berlin just to catch up. That's a huge journey.' 'It is indeed,' she replies. 'I was quite shocked at how long it took. But just think how marvellous it will be to make the next part of the journey together. All the while I've been overjoyed at the thought of travelling in your company!'
>
> She stands in the middle of the room, dressed in her great-coat with its big collar, in her hand her pink straw hat which she is so proud of, but we all find quite awful!
>
> 'Lyolya, you're an odd shape, what have you got in your pockets?' 'Oh that!' she replies enthusiastically. 'I mislaid my travelling bag, but was so pleased to find that my coat pockets were so big I could put my overnight things in them.'

---

[53] Hunnius, *Mein Weg zur Kunst*, p. 253.

With shrieks of laughter and amazement we help her to empty her pockets.
There are all sorts! First up, her nightgown. 'That was the most difficult to get
in,' she says. Then follows a bar of soap, a comb, a toothbrush, a sponge
wrapped in paper, now quite damp, then a host of bits and pieces which she
had gathered up at the last minute and stuffed into her pockets.

'Oh, Lyolya, you can't be left alone for a single minute!' I tell her.

'I quite agree,' she responds 'That's why I'm so glad we're all together
once more!'[54]

Kashperova could have travelled home from Königsberg to St Petersburg
directly, a distance of 650 km, in a matter of hours. Her spontaneous detour
via Berlin entailed a round trip of 2,400 km.

Since graduating from the Conservatoire in 1895, there is further evidence that
Kashperova had acquired a sizeable reputation and gained both respect and
affection. This much can be gleaned from the entry for 26 March 1906 in the
memoirs of V. V. Yastrebtsev (Rimsky-Korsakov's biographer). It concerns a visit
paid to the great composer. Yastrebtsev comments that the previous evening he
had attended 'a performance of Kashperova's cello sonata [and] all of her songs to
her own texts', surely referring to the twelve *Songs of Love*.[55] In reply to
Yastrebtsev's observation that Kashperova's compositions displayed an 'uncom-
mon musicality', Rimsky is reported to have remarked that Solovyov too was
extremely impressed with the talents of his former student 'and had nicknamed
her *Snow Maiden*', after Rimsky-Korsakov's opera (1881, rev. 1895).

1907

Besides her concert activities, Kashperova maintained a busy schedule of piano
teaching, over time acquiring a considerable following of admirers and friends.
This is reflected in the fact that her many pupils united to offer their assistance –
indeed, to provide sufficient financial support to enable Kashperova to resign
from her salaried post at the St Petersburg Music School and to embark upon
several concert tours abroad; at least three are recorded. (After one year of such
excursions, however, as her *Memoirs* relate, she did not feel comfortable calling
upon such generosity again.) In 1907, she performed her piano concerto in
Berlin.[56] Kashperova's first recital in London took place in the Aeolian Hall on
6 June 1907 and included her Piano Trio in D, op. 3 performed with Jan
Hambourg on violin and Boris Hambourg on violoncello. She was accommo-
dated in Dorset Square, Marylebone, its elegant Regency architecture surely

[54] Ibid., pp. 256–7.
[55] Cited in Kashperova, *Vospominaniya*, p. 136. Source given as: Nikolai Andreyevich Rimsky-
Korsakov, *The Memoirs of V. V. Yastrebstev*. vol. 2 (Leningrad: 1960), p. 382.
[56] No details are yet available beyond mention in Kashperova, *Vospominaniya*, p. 135.

reminding her of the mansion at Bochatino some 3,000 km distant. The *Sunday Times* would note approvingly that she was a pupil of Anton Rubinstein, observing that

> she bears out the tradition that the great man forbade the principle of imitation in his teaching, [for] her playing testifies to an innate independence of spirit. Reflective and very refined, the pianist perhaps was at her best in her softer phrases where her touch and tone were delicate and delightful; yet her style is not without moments of fire – though these are intellectual and deliberate rather than emotional. As a composer, Mlle Kashperow shows a decided talent, and her Trio [in D, op. 3] in which she was associated with Messrs. Jan and Boris Hambourg was received with marked favour. It is lengthy [surely in four movements] but very attractive in its tunefulness, grace, and Russian fitfulness of mood.[57]

Her recital in Leipzig, however, was given a hostile review in the *Musikalischen Wochenblatts* (17 October 1907). The critic took exception to Kashperova's G major Cello Sonata, op. 1, no. 1 (referred to, erroneously, as being in F major). Apparently, this 'did not in any way correspond to the demands of chamber music style, for the piano part is far too *concertante* and invasive'. Disappointed, the writer further criticises the work for its 'unadorned salon-genre characterised by its empty rhetoric ... though the Scherzo is lively and amusing'. In contrast, the playing of the (Leipzig-based) cellist Heinrich Grünfeld is highly praised, though 'what a pity that such artistry should be wasted on such nothingness ['an ein Nichts'].' As for Kashperova's piano playing this was 'not without errors ... and suffered from an often dubious choice of overhasty tempo'. So disagreeable was this critic's experience that he opted to leave the concert before the end, though not before suffering the embarrassment of bumping into the 'Komponistin Kashperow' on the stairs in his haste to exit.

Kashperova presented her second London recital on Tuesday afternoon 22 October 1907 at the Queen's Hall. Her performance was reviewed in the *Violin Times* in the following terms: '[This] pupil of Rubinstein ... gave proof of neat and exact technique, a fine tone and clear touch. She was heard in compositions by Chopin, Lyadov, Schumann and Rubinstein.' The review continued: 'Jean Gérardy [the Belgian cellist who, as a student, had performed in a trio with Ysaÿe and Paderewski] was to have taken the cello part in a Sonata [by Kashperova] for piano and cello, but he was prevented from doing so by indisposition.'[58] To fill the gap, Kashperova performed her as yet unpublished *In the Midst of Nature*. The critic of the *Musical Standard* reported that Kashperova had 'won the admiration of musicians'.[59]

[57] Newspaper cutting held at the Russian National Museum of Music, Moscow: Archive 345/ 210.
[58] *Violin Times* (London), December 1907, p. 177.
[59] *Musical Standard* (London), 2 November 1907, p. 279.

Back in St Petersburg, however, she had unwittingly become the target of some bitter criticism from Balakirev (with whom she would later work harmoniously). For now, however, they had clearly never met. He had been lent a score of her Symphony by César Cui who, judging from previous commentaries, was probably impressed by it and wished to share this enthusiasm with his illustrious colleague. However, Balakirev's letter (8 May 1907)[60] accompanying the return of the score makes abundantly clear his distaste for Kashperova's stylistic and technical idiosyncrasies, for they ran contrary to his rigid view of what should constitute a true Russian work of the nationalist school:

> I cannot deny that fact that she has talent, but the lack of efficient guidance makes this composition untenable. Its orchestration is weak. In particular, her constant and unnecessary pursuit of solos [*sic*] harms her work. If Kashperova is not old can you advise her to work hard on the form of composition and on orchestration under the guidance of a capable composer like Lyadov?

Balakirev was clearly unaware that Kashperova had rejected guidance from Lyadov twelve years earlier. Meanwhile, a more fundamental issue was taxing the ever-critical Balakirev. 'If you get the opportunity,' he finishes his letter to Cui, 'you can ask her where she got the name Leokadiya from (if she is Russian). We do not have such a name. She must be a Catholic or a Pole, judging by the name.' His implied objection to her Polish-ness is surprising for, despite his xenophobic tendencies, Balakirev admired Chopin profoundly; his catalogue is full of Polish references and Chopin-esque genres including Impromptus, Preludes, Waltzes, Scherzos, a Tarantella and several Mazurkas.

1908

Russian musicologist Tatiana Zaytseva has informed the author (in conversation in April 2014) that although Balakirev was critical of Kashperova for her Chopin interpretation, he did approve of her sparing use of the sustaining pedal in accordance with his own taste. Kashperova's approach to sonority and the use of the pedal were clearly unusual and individual. In fact, judging from Kashperova's recommendation to young pianists that they learn from those such as Moritz Rosenthal (1862–1946; see Section 3), she clearly based her own playing upon pianistic traditions that valued clarity of texture, an approach that finds its origin and justification in Chopin's own teaching. Rosenthal had studied with Chopin's pupil Karol Mikuli, who was also noted for his sparing use of the pedal. In 1908, Kashperova performed Balakirev's Piano Sonata no. 2, developing such an affinity with this work that she would go on to record the

---

[60] Cui, *Избранные письма* [*Selected Letters*], letter XLI, p. 522, note, p. 714.

Музыкальный вечер у М. А. Балакирева, 1908 г.

Figure 2 'A Musical Evening at M. A. Balakirev's, 1908'. Seated, left to right: M. A. Balakirev, L. A. Kashperova, S. M. Lyapunov. Standing, left to right: J. G. Zimmerman, B. L. Zhilinsky, M. P. Karlov, A. Y. Zimmerman.
Image: *courtesy of Dr. Tatiana A. Zaytseva (St Petersburg Conservatoire).*

sonata for the Welte-Mignon Company in 1910. Over time – in response, perhaps, to Kashperova's growing admiration for his music – Balakirev developed a respect for her versatile talents and a productive working relationship was established. In a letter (27 May 1909) held in the manuscripts department of the Russian National Library, she thanks him for his 'promise to assist' her in making the piano transcription of her Symphony.[61] She was even photographed with Balakirev seated at the centre of his illustrious inner circle (see Figure 2).

On Sunday 20 April, Aleksandr Verzhbilovich and Kashperova presented a recital in the Maly Zal (Small Hall) of the St Petersburg Conservatoire. The programme was constructed around her own compositions and included the premiere of her Cello Sonata no. 3 in F. This was enthusiastically received by the critic of the *Mährisches Tagblatt* who also praised the *Russian Serenade* for its effective imitations of the balalaika.[62] Evidently this had to be repeated

---

[61] Russian National Library, Ostrovskogo Square, St Petersburg: Manuscripts department/ Balakirev archive/Kashperova collection/1909.

[62] Regrettably this work, too, is lost.

as did 'The Threshing of the Wheat', the final movement of her suite for piano *In The Midst of Nature*.[63]

1909–1910

On 2 March 1909, Kashperova gave the first performance of Balakirev's Symphony no. 2 in D minor (1908) with Sergei Lyapunov (b. Yaroslavl, 1859–1924) in the composer's four-hand arrangement. The Symphony was subsequently premiered as an orchestral work at a Free School concert on 23 April under Lyapunov's direction.

Kashperova's Romantic empathy with nature and childhood has already been noted, particularly in her settings of Polonsky's verses *The Eagle and the Snake* and the mystical 'legend' (in its original title) *In Reply to a Child's Question: Where Do The Stars Come From?* The six-movement piano suite *In the Midst of Nature* of 1910 is also typical in its evocation of nature, here suggesting Kashperova's nostalgia for her childhood spent in the pastoral surroundings of the family estate at Bochatino. As an adult based in St Petersburg she would look forward eagerly to returning every summer to reacquaint herself with its 'parkland of lime trees leading down the slope of the hill to the Shacha river valley'.[64] *In the Midst of Nature* is dedicated to her younger sister Elizaveta and presents an artfully graded progression, suggesting that Kashperova probably shared this music with her many pupils: the early movements are within the range of the talented young player whilst the latter movements require the technique and interpretative maturity of a more advanced student.

Russian audiences in particular would have identified with these vividly descriptive portraits: the first 'Rose' appears to be a fond memory of the garden at Bochatino as described by Kashperova in her memoirs. The second 'Rose' is more purposeful, as if accompanying the narration of a Russian folktale. The 'Two Autumn Leaves' are similarly contrasted: the first evokes the stillness of autumn, perhaps the falling of leaves settling upon the surface of a garden pond, gently circling in all their varied colours and reflections. The second suggests the wind in the trees blowing the leaves into the air with ever-increasing gusto. The Bochatino estate is surrounded by vast expanses of rye and wheat; the young 'Lyolya' and her siblings must have enjoyed wading through the tall grasses on a windy day imagining they could hear 'The Murmuring of the Rye'. The final movement presents a different mood altogether. In graphic, almost mocking terms, it seems to depict the industrialisation of agriculture via the noisy invasion of the peaceful Russian landscape. 'The Threshing of the Wheat'

---

[63] Kashperova retained a copy of the review, now held in the Kashperova archive: 345/211.

[64] T. V. Voytuk-Jensen, 'The Susaninsky Empire'. Translation: P. John Shepherd (2020). Information received from the Academic Library of Kostroma Region, 23 March 2020.

is depicted in two ways. First, in terms of rhythmic energy suggestive of agricultural machinery whose functioning is far from smooth: the motor evidently requires some vigorous turns of the crank handle before exploding into action. At the end it appears to splutter and break down in dramatic, comic fashion. The contrasting middle section suggests a moment of rest, of prayer even, perhaps in the olden style: the peasant workforce sinking to their knees in devout chant to offer up grateful thanks for the abundant harvest; then rising again to sing and dance before returning to their strenuous labours.

Kashperova would later describe a typical domestic scene on the garden steps overlooking the birch-forest. 'In the evening,' she writes in her memoirs, 'the whole family sits outside. A group of peasants returns home from the fields, singing as they pass by.' Stravinsky recalls a similar scene at the family dacha at Ustilug.[65] Such nostalgia might well have prompted the composition of *In the Midst of Nature*.

It is possible that 1910 was also the year of a recital reviewed by César Cui marking a visit to St Petersburg by the distinguished violinist František Ondříček (1857–1922), the dedicatee of Dvorak's Violin Concerto (1883). He is accompanied by Kashperova, whom Cui describes as: 'one of our most talented young pianists. She possesses remarkable technique, and her performances are unfailingly alive and musical. Despite the presence of the imposing Ondříček she had great and well-deserved success. Especially artistic was her rendering of Liszt's [Schubert transcription] *Du bist die Ruh*' which she was asked to encore'.[66]

While Kashperova's individuality as a recitalist was consistently praised in this way – in London, one recalls, the *Sunday Times* reviewer had appreciated her 'innately independent spirit' – there is surprisingly little evidence of a parallel career as a concerto soloist, as one might surely expect from a performer of her calibre (with the rare exceptions of her own Piano Concerto and Rubinstein's fifth, both now distant memories). It seems that in an orchestral context this same individuality – described by Maikapar euphemistically, one suspects, as her 'extraordinary directness' – may have been an impediment. Kashperova is described as a 'huge risk' by Josef Borovka, director of the St Petersburg Music School where Kashperova had once taught. Borovka warns Balakirev not to include her in his plans for the upcoming Chopin centenary concert in March 1910 because 'she does not recognise any leadership [i.e. direction from the conductor] and wants to stay independent of this ... She will do such mischief in the [*Rondo à la*] *Krakowiak* that you will not be able to manage her.'[67]

[65] Stravinsky, *An Autobiography*, p. 4.

[66] Cui, *Избранные письма* (Selected Letters), pp. 209–10 (text undated).

[67] T. A. Zaytseva & A. G. Petropavlov eds., *Наше святое ремесло* (Our Hallowed Craft – Memories of V. V. Nilsen, 1910–98), (St Petersburg Conservatoire, 2004), pp. 299–300. The centenary

In 1910, Welte-Mignon transported its recording equipment from Freiburg to Russia and invited several distinguished pianists, Skryabin and Glazunov amongst them, to register their compositions. Kashperova recorded *In the Midst of Nature*; also Balakirev's Sonata no. 2 in B Minor and a Prelude by Cui.[68] Rare, possibly unique copies of these piano rolls are held in London, at the Musical Museum in Brentford.[69]

1912

Kashperova's reputation as a chamber musician was never greater. She is the subject of a lengthy review published in the *Russkaya Muzikal'naya Gazyeta* ('Russian Musical Gazette') whose remit included regular coverage of the city's most significant chamber music concerts. Issue no. 16 of 15 April 1912 carries several reviews of recitals by celebrated Russian musicians; these include Skryabin giving the first performance in St Petersburg of his recently-composed Sonata no. 7 'White Mass', and a concert by the eleven-year-old prodigy Jascha Heifetz. Also reviewed is a 'Clavierabend' given by Kashperova on 3 April. It is an indication of the scarcity of Kashperova-related documents relevant to the second half of her life and career, that this is the last-dated review *so far uncovered* that mentions Kashperova. For this reason, and for marking the premiere of two mature compositions (regrettably untraced at the time of this publication), it is worth quoting extensively:

> [Kashperova's recital] was of considerable interest mainly because of the performance of two new compositions by this talented pianist: the Trio for piano, viola [*sic*] and cello and seven piano pieces [entitled] *Hommage aux œuvres de Pietro Canonica*. The Trio is dedicated to the memory of A. V. Verzhbilovich [d. 1911] and although the mood is gloomy and mournful the music is not sentimental, no sweet sighs or nostalgia. Instead, the score conveys a strong and convincing individuality. Of particular note are the two final movements (out of four): the Scherzo and the Theme & Variations

concert would include performances of Balakirev's *Zelazowa Wola,* and *Chopin Suite* conducted by Lyapunov.

[68] See 'Balakirev Piano Sonata in B flat Minor Played by Leokadiya Kashperova', YouTube video www.youtube.com/watch?v=ePaWef3WYdQ&t=67s. This was produced by Julian Dyer with the support of Denis Hall and the Pianola Institute.

[69] The piano roll of *In the Midst of Nature* remains in a private collection in Italy. See *Catalogue of Compositions* for further details. It is regrettable that Welte-Mignon did not return to Russia in 1912 and record *Hommage aux œuvres de Pietro Canonica*, to register this mature work for posterity. (The score remains lost.) At the time of going to press it is not known how these piano rolls came to be archived in Brentford. Similarly unknown is the provenance of a copy of Kashperova's Symphony, which is held in the Sir Thomas Beecham Collection (Western Bank Library) at Sheffield University. It is possible, if not highly likely, that the composer intentionally left this score at the Queen's Hall on the occasion of her recital there in 1907, the same year that Beecham founded his New Symphony Orchestra based at the Queen's Hall.

are written with an excellent sense of sonority between the instruments and with some impressive contrapuntal effects. Seven sculptural creations by Pietro Canonica [1869–1959] served as the inspiration for Kashperova's 'sound pictures' which include 'Armonia d'anima', 'Primavera' and 'Aurora ridente'. This is beautiful music, skilfully written and graceful. In conclusion, let us affirm that the talent of Mlle Kashperova as a composer is undoubtedly a gratifying phenomenon of St Petersburg's musical life.

The 'impressive contrapuntal effects' surely reflect Kashperova's affinity with canonic writing, as she herself recognised and commented upon at the Conservatoire in conversation with fellow-student Samuel Maikapar (whom she regarded as better than her at writing fugues). The review provides the only known evidence of Kashperova writing a Theme & Variations movement. The positive response to the Scherzo would suggest she already enjoyed a reputation as a brilliant creator of fast and witty Scherzos – as can be witnessed in her two early Cello Sonatas and the Symphony and, still to come, in the posthumous Piano Trio.

Three weeks after this momentous concert, allowing time for the 1,000 km journey to Kostroma (where the Kashperov family spent the winter months), Leokadiya participated in a chamber music recital in the city's elegant Assembly Rooms. It was attended, surely 'filled to the rafters', by friends and family members as well as by city dignitaries for Kostroma now boasted regular concerts along the lines of the Russian Musical Society. She performed the music of Chopin (a Nocturne and Ballade, unspecified), Rubinstein's Violin Sonata no. 1 in G, op. 13 (with B. A. Mikhailovsky) and, in conclusion, evoking the surrounding countryside so familiar to her audience, she performed four movements from *In the Midst of Nature*: 'Two Roses', 'The Murmuring of the Rye' and the ever-popular 'The Threshing of the Wheat'.

1916–1917

One recalls that upon her graduation from the St Petersburg Conservatoire Kashperova was granted the title of Free Artist. This enabled her to seek employment in the best educational establishments in the city. According to Fesenkova, in her introduction to the memoirs, Kashperova initially 'taught piano at the J. A. Borovka [he of the 'huge risk'] music school', referring to the St Petersburg Music School (founded in 1887) on Nevsky Prospect no. 16, where she taught for many years.[70] Later, from January to September 1916, she

---

[70] A colleague of Kashperova's at the St Petersburg Music School from 1908 was the pianist Nikolai (Ivanovich) Richter (1879–1944). He was later appointed a professor at the Conservatoire. Richter was the dedicatee of Stravinsky's early *Scherzo* (1902) and gave the first performance of the Sonata in F# Minor (1903–4) which Stravinsky composed under the supervision of Rimsky-Korsakov.

was employed as a piano teacher at the Smolny Institute,[71] which had been founded in 1764 as the 'Imperial Training College for Daughters of the Nobility'. In a letter marked 'Petrograd 29 February 1916', Kashperova also applied to teach at the palatial Pavlovsky Institute ('Tsar Paul's Institute').[72] She received a reply the following month addressing her as Elikonida and, somewhat curiously, confirming her 'husband's name' as S. V. Andropov, even though they were married only later that year, on 25 September.[73] Kashperova would later recall that when she first met her future husband, 'I did not know of his extraordinary revolutionary activities [but] I immediately noticed that here was a man of exceptional abilities and, on closer acquaintance, I was impressed by his erudition. Everything that interested him he mastered in depth. He was fluent in four languages, and in music I could only marvel at his broad understanding and his memory.' Consideration of Andropov at this point is more than of merely passing relevance, for Kashperova's life changed dramatically from the moment of her first encounter with this evidently captivating and highly cultured professional revolutionary.[74]

Sergei Vasilyevich Andropov (8/20 October 1873–January 1956) was born in the south in Novocherkassk, historically the centre of Don Cossack heritage and culture. While a student at St Petersburg University in 1898 he had organised a strike at the Maxwell textile factory. He was arrested and sentenced to eight years of exile in Eastern Siberia from where he managed to escape after four months.[75] He rose to become a high-ranking Soviet engineer and propagandist and is mentioned several times in Lenin's correspondence.[76] His audacious activities, printing and distributing the pro-revolutionary newspaper *Iskra* ('The Spark'), led to his arrest by Tsarist police and imprisonment in St Petersburg's Peter and Paul Fortress on several occasions. There, in 1901 for example (the year Kashperova premiered her Piano Concerto), he spent over twelve months in solitary confinement before being given a ten-year sentence and deported to the Achinsk region, east of the Ural mountains. From there he fled to Geneva to

---

[71] Cf. correspondence held at the Central Historical State Archive of St Petersburg: Archive 2, Inventory 1, File 18996.

[72] Ibid.: Archive 2/Inventory 1/File 18996.

[73] Ibid.: Archive 7/Inventory 2/File 1793. A copy of the wedding invitation is held at the Russian National Music of Music, Moscow: Archive 345/172.

[74] Y. A. Yoselev, 'An Agent of Lenin's *Iskra*' – from the series *Professional Revolutionaries* (information provided by the Library of the Rostov-on-Don Conservatoire, via email 20 November 2015).

[75] Cf. 'Andropov Sergei Vasilievich' at www.geni.com

[76] Lenin records in his diary that he helped Andropov publish *The Workers Banner* and supported his *Iskra* ('The Spark') activities from 1901. Novikov, V. I., *Ленин и деятельность искровских групп в России (1900-1903)* [*Lenin and the Activities of the Iskra Groups in Russia (1900–1903)*] (Moscow: 'Thought' Press, 1984).

meet again with Lenin and receive further assignments. More arrests and imprisonments followed, with deportations to ever more distant exile, even to Yenisei Ostrog [stockade] in Northeastern Siberia. He managed to escape from captivity repeatedly and make his way to his maternal home in Switzerland.[77] This would have necessitated journeys, presumably for the most part on foot, of several thousand kilometres.[78] In due course Andropov travelled to Germany where he enrolled at Heidelberg University in 1911. Later he resided in London where, under the pseudonym Albyn, he operated an underground printing press with a fellow revolutionary 'factory worker' V. P. Nogin. Viktor Nogin later rose to the very top of the Bolshevik Party in Moscow and is buried in Red Square. Together, they would continue the *Iskra* operation started by Lenin himself in 1902 (at 37a Clerkenwell Green, EC1) receiving only food as payment. In 1916 Andropov returned to Russia, and upon his arrival in St Peterburg he commenced piano lessons with Kashperova. His uncle had been 'inspector of music' at the Don Ladies Institute for Noble Maidens in Rostov-on-Don and was a 'composer of salon pieces' for piano. Andropov, it seems, had 'always been interested in music'.[79]

Immediately following her marriage to Sergei Andropov in September 1916, and as social unrest increased, Kashperova wrote again to the Smolny and Pavlovsky Institutes, this time announcing her immediate resignation from these bastions of tradition and privilege. The Smolny Institute, for example, had been founded by Catherine the Great to provide education to the daughters of the Russian nobility, or 'noble maidens' as this is often charmingly translated. Not only were the young pupils titled, but many were also princesses. St Petersburg's Russian Museum contains a gallery of portraits by Dmitri Levitsky (1735–1822) of the most celebrated Smolyanki, as they were known, busily occupying themselves with such aristocratic pastimes as dancing (note the balletic pose of Natalia Borshcheva who at fifteen had already caught the eye of Tsar Paul I) or harp-playing or, more surprisingly, science (note Ekaterina Molchanova, book in hand, engaged in scientific experiments in an effort, it is said, to emulate the latest advances in Paris).[80]

---

[77] Andropov's mother was the daughter of the prominent Swiss architect Karl Aeschlimann (1808–93), responsible for many of the Crimea's most elegant seafront mansions.

[78] Achinsk is located 4,300 km east of St Petersburg: from there to Geneva would have entailed a journey of 6,420 km. Yenisei is located 5,200 km east of St Petersburg: from there to Geneva is 7,250 km.

[79] Information provided by the Library of the Conservatoire of Rostov-on-Don, via email 30/11/2015. See also the Russian genealogy website: www.famhist.ru/famhist/klasson/0002a456.htm#00003095.htm (accessed 1 May 2021).

[80] See link to the Russian Museum: http://en.rusmuseum.ru/benois-wing/exhibitions/smolyanki-by-dmitry-levitsky-to-the-275th-anniversary-of-the-artist-s-birth/?sphrase_id=265443#rmPhoto [gallery3265]/6/.

Initial research suggested that Kashperova had been coerced into resigning from these highly valued teaching posts under pressure from her agitprop husband, keen to avoid explaining to his Bolshevik colleagues where his new wife was employed. However, one should also consider the possibility that Andropov might have had a premonition, if not inside knowledge, that impelled him to act swiftly and to extract his bride from this potentially hazardous, if not actually life-threatening, association. If this were the case, then by so doing he surely saved her from grave danger. Upon Lenin's arrival in Petrograd in April 1917 the Smolny Institute was immediately closed down and its palatial neo-classical buildings co-opted as the command centre of the Bolshevik Party. It was there that the victory of the Revolution was proclaimed and where Lenin established his headquarters; and where Kirov would be assassinated in 1934.

One cannot underestimate the Revolution's bewildering impact upon young women such as Kashperova's young pupils (and upon Kashperova herself) as the following examples from opposite ends of the social spectrum illustrate. First, a widely held account of events at the Smolny Institute on the day after the Tsar's abdication (15 March 1917). For the first time in three centuries there was to be no prayer for the Tsar and his family. The young student chosen to lead the assembly that morning broke down, it is said, unable to pronounce 'Let us pray for the Provisional Government', provoking all pupils and staff present to join her in tears and sobbing. Second, history recalls the role of Orthodox priests in Moscow's Red Square blessing the newly formed 'Women's Battalion of Death' soon to be sent to the front line in a ploy designed to shame the Russian army into more manly, more patriotic action. Both images are poign-antly expressive of that immense upheaval, of such violence prevalent in so many forms amidst the chaos caused by the catastrophic and simultaneous impact of war, revolution and civil war upon Russian society.

1918–1922

Information about Kashperova in Russian literature is minimal, largely restricted to addenda at the foot of expansive lexicon entries about Vladimir Kashperov.[81] For the most part, these brief references describe Kashperova as 'a pianist and teacher' with no mention of 'composer'. Perhaps, as is likely, the editors had never heard her music performed or did not know of her compos-itions – or thought that the notion of a female composer was, to coin a phrase, 'just a farcical idea'.[82] One Soviet publication, however, confidently states that

---

[81] It is up to future researchers to fill in the details of Kashperova's transition from Petrograd to Moscow via Rostov-on-Don. Indeed, her entire biography requires amplification and refinement, as will surely come to pass in time.

[82] A reference to Rubinstein's view of women conductors. See Section 3.

'from 1918–1922 Kashperova taught at the Conservatoire in Rostov-on-Don',[83] capital of that southern region hauntingly described in Mikhail Sholokhov's portrait of the Don Cossacks' struggles during the Russian Civil War: *And Quietly Flows the Don*. However, when the present author contacted the Rostov Conservatoire in 2015 (there has been no opportunity to travel there since then) the librarians could find no record of Kashperova having worked in Rostov, although they succeeded in providing information about Sergei Andropov, for which I am very grateful. All that can be confirmed for the present is that by the end of 1918 Kashperova and her husband had left Petrograd;[84] and in such haste that her recent scores were left behind, disastrously so. The couple's initial destination may well have been Rostov-on-Don, where Andropov had both roots and 'history' for it was there that he had participated in the armed uprisings of December 1905.[85] Indeed, for that reason, he may have been posted back to his home region on official revolutionary business (rather than 'flee' Petrograd, as was suggested earlier) and decided on a whim to install his bride quickly in a familiar and relatively safe haven far from the epicentre of revolution. It is likely that wherever she found herself Kashperova would want, and need, to continue working. She would therefore have sought opportunities to teach and to perform in the south.[86] According to Fesenkova (writing in 1968) she relocated to Moscow in 1922.[87] Over the course of the next eighteen years, until her death in 1940, Kashperova struggled to maintain her musical career whilst her husband worked successfully for several of the capital's most important political and economic organisations. Andropov rose to elevated positions at the Supreme Council of National Economy, the Communist International ('Comintern'), the Marx-Engels-Lenin Institute, the People's Commissariat of the Textile Industry (working alongside Viktor Nogin), and at the Main Astronomical Observatory. He also taught mathematics, his specialism, to Red Army commanders within the Kremlin.

On 30 November 1920, whilst still based in Rostov-on-Don, Kashperova visited Moscow to give an all-Beethoven recital at the Maly Zal ('small auditorium'). The concert poster (See Figure D: www.cambridge.org/Graham_Online appendix) announces the now-married pianist as 'L. A. Kashperova-Andropova', re-named

---

[83] G. B. Bernhardt and I. M. Yampolsky, *Кто писпл о музыке* [*Who Wrote about Music*] (Leningrad: All Union Publishers Sovyetsky Kompozitor, 1974), p. 73.

[84] Kashperova, *Vospominaniya*, p. 136.

[85] After the disruptions of 1905 Andropov fled to Odessa where he set up an underground press and published the Marxist pamphlet 'The Railway Worker'. When the press was raided in 1907 he moved to St Petersburg where he continued his underground activities.

[86] This has yet to be confirmed.

[87] Fesenkova's introduction to Kashperova, *Vospominaniya*, p. 136.

according to Russian custom. The event was an impressive professional landmark that promised so much for her future career in the Russian capital. It is notable too for its extraordinarily demanding programme and offers the clearest indication available of the elevated artistry that her pianism demonstrated by this time. Kashperova performed, in sequence, Beethoven's last four sonatas: opp. 106 ('Das Hammerklavier'), 109, 110 and 111. Evidently not one for a trifling encore, she concluded the banquet with op. 81a. Kashperova would surely have explained to her audience (as is the Russian custom to this day) that this was her personal acknowledgement to Rubinstein, who had often confided to his students that *Les Adieux* was 'close to his heart'. According to her *Recollections* he had also 'taken his students through the late sonatas with especial affection'.

The recital was also deeply significant for marking another, more devastating, 'farewell'. Having announced her arrival in Moscow in such style, Kashperova could not possibly have imagined that her all-Beethoven programme would effectively bring the curtain down prematurely on her career. Never again did she perform a solo recital. Thereafter, until her death in 1940, she made only rare appearances, mostly in collective concerts – for example, to perform the music of the old guard, Glazunov or Balakirev or Lyapunov or Rubinstein, or in entertainments designed to celebrate regional folk music of the Soviet republics. At the age of forty-eight, at the height of her pianistic and interpretative powers, she was effectively silenced; indeed, silenced twice, as a concert-pianist *and as a composer*. Except for a few songs it seems that not a note of her own music was ever performed again in her lifetime.[88]

1928–1929

Despite such musical and professional deprivations, Kashperova would have found some consolation from her regular involvement with Moscow's chamber music community. On 21 November 1928, as Kashperova-Andropova, she participated in a Schubert Evening at the House of Learning on Kropotkin Street.[89] On 6 October 1929, she performed with L. T. Merkulova (singer) and E. V. Davidova (piano) in a recital promoted by the Moscow Chamber Music Association including 'Songs and Piano Sonatas by Balakirev, Lyapunov and Glazunov'.[90] On 21 November, surely marking the centenary of the birth of Anton Rubinstein (28 November 1829), the Moscow Chamber Music

---

[88] Nor in subsequent decades since her death, until the author's lecture-recital at the St Petersburg Conservatoire on 27 October 2015, when the Scherzo from the Symphony in B Minor and *In the Midst of Nature* (complete) were discussed and performed.

[89] Concert flyer held at the Russian National Museum of Music, Moscow. Archive 345/61.

[90] Ibid.: Archive 345/63.

Association presented Kashperova-Andropova with several other musicians (three singers, a cellist, another four pianists) in a programme that included Rubinstein's 'songs, his cello sonata and Trio'.[91]

Although there is no documentary evidence to support this, it is possible that after her arrival in Moscow Kashperova would have contacted her relative Elizaveta (Vladimirovna) Kashperova (1871–1945), the daughter of the opera composer Vladimir Kashperov. Elizaveta had recently been appointed piano teacher at the Conservatoire.[92] Indeed, such an encounter is very likely for Leokadiya and her husband soon moved into an apartment directly opposite the Conservatoire, at Bolshoya Nikitskaya ulitsa no. 14/5 (see Figure 3).[93] However Soviet policy, officially at least, was to disapprove of nepotism in any form; this would have deterred any attempt to create a post for Kashperova at the Conservatoire. She must surely have continued to teach the piano privately, in her apartment or elsewhere in Moscow. Gone forever was the hard-earned and elevated status she had previously enjoyed. Clearly, she could not remind a soul of her former high standing in 'good old St Petersburg'. Nor would it have been wise to attempt to impress the authorities with tales of the positive reception she had been afforded in the capitalist West, in Berlin and on her two visits to London. Furthermore, she was of noble birth – a major drawback after the Revolution; it was far safer to keep a low profile.

Kashperova continued to compose, though her output was small in scale compared with earlier years. She completed a number of short piano solos and duets and songs, probably written for her students. Her life-long interest in poetry is reflected in the wide range of Russian authors chosen to provide the lyrics to her settings: these include Balmont, Esenin, Nikitin, Koltsov, Strakhov and Krylov, as well as, of course, Polonsky. Kashperova continued to set her own poetic texts. In 1924, to mark the solemn occasion (and written very possibly at her husband's request), she composed *On the Death of Lenin,* intended for performance by the '9th Children's Colony at the Pushkin Settlement' – to her own lyrics. It begins: 'We gathered in a sad crowd to honour the memory of a genius … '[94]

---

[91] Ibid.: Archive 345/59.

[92] Elizaveta Kashperova studied at the Moscow Conservatoire (1885–92) alongside Rakhmaninov and taught there from 1921 to 1931. Her compositions include art-songs and piano solos (cf. Boosey & Hawkes, London). She worked as 'concert organiser at steel plants' in southern Russia (1898–1913) and for Proletkult in Moscow (1918–21). (Information kindly provided by Russian genealogist Tatiana Molchanova – email to the author, 22 April 2019.)

[93] The street was formerly called Aleksandr Herzen ulitsa. Today, the Kashperova apartment is situated opposite the entrance to the Moscow Conservatoire's 'Rakhmaninov Concert Hall'.

[94] 'I can't listen to music too often,' Lenin once admitted after hearing a performance of Beethoven's *Appassionata* Sonata. 'It makes me want to say kind, stupid things, and pat the

Figure 3 The Moscow address where L. A. Kashperova resided from ca. 1922
to her death in 1940: Aleksandr Herzen ulitsa 14, Kvartira 5 (Herzen Street 14,
apartment 5). It is situated almost directly opposite the Moscow Conservatoire.
The street has since been renamed Bolshoya Nikitskaya ulitsa. Kashperova's
apartment is on the first floor: the 4th, 5th and 6th windows from the right
(above the 'Koffee-bean' café: Кофебин).
Image: Graham Griffiths (2016)

The impact of the Revolution began to spread deeper into the Russian
hinterland, eventually to collide with the remote and once-peaceful family
mansion at Bochatino. The director of the Kostroma Museum visited the estate
in 1928 to find that the property had been ransacked, 'the railings taken apart,
door locks and brackets torn out, most of the windows broken, the roof leaking,
the plaster falling off the walls, the park's centuries-old [forest] largely felled. In
a word, a special site in the English Regency style, unique of its kind, has
perished'.[95] When Kashperova heard of this devastation she was understand-
ably prompted to recall happier times, particularly so after her mother's death in
1929: by the end of that year she had set down her memoirs, which record her
joyous family upbringing of roses, rye and wheat – also 'preserved' *sub rosa*

---

heads of people. But now you have to beat them on the head, beat them without mercy.' Cited in
     Orlando Figes, *Revolutionary Russia, 1891–1991* (London: Pelican Books, 2014), p. 23.
[95] T. V. Voytuk-Jensen, 'The Susaninsky Empire', trans. P. John Shepherd (2020). The derelict
     ruins of Bochatino were cleared in 1939 to make way for the construction of a cheese factory.

through her music (see Section 2). The chronological narration of the *Memoirs* breaks off around 1907, soon after that fateful year of the first Russian revolution (1905). Her typescript ends tamely, innocently, though (for today's reader) with the shock of understatement. She was surely conscious of the necessity of avoiding recriminations to herself and to others with careless mention of names – as was Stravinsky, whose 1935 autobiography avoids mention of Kashperova and others by name. She signs off simply, disarmingly: 'On Tuesday evenings I had musical evenings at home. My life was completely full'. What happened in subsequent years Kashperova chose not to divulge. Her life was 'completely full'. Yet, that literary smile barely conceals a numbed sadness. The apparently serene, somewhat distant, seemingly happy *Memoirs* convey her weary regret and, as she looked out of her front window at the Conservatoire opposite, her bitter frustration at the utter collapse of her professional life.

1930–1940

In 2016 I was prompted by the head of the Moscow Conservatoire library to visit the Glinka State Consortium of Musical Culture with the purpose of investigating an archive which 'might be of interest'.[96] (To Irina Torilova I offer my deepest gratitude.) This unexpected encounter with 230 files of Kashperova materials represented a seismic breakthrough, particularly so as library records showed that no one had opened archive no. 345 since it had been catalogued in 1971, its subterranean hibernation undisturbed for forty-five years (see Acknowledgements). Importantly, the collection revealed that amidst the assorted documents, cuttings, photos and half-finished musical sketches, Kashperova had also left behind a small number of nearly completed compositions in faint manuscript. Their fading pencil note-heads (the tiniest of dots) would require much determined editing but given time it would be possible to bring these precious scores to print.

The first complete work to be uncovered and restored was a setting of two short Polonsky poems *Evening & Night*. Kashperova greatly admired the music of Sergei Taneyev (1856–1915) and might well have been drawn to these verses after hearing Taneyev's setting of them within his *Twelve Choruses*, op. 27 for SATB choir, composed in 1909. Kashperova's decision to write for female voices only (SSAA) may reflect the positive memories of her summer-school experience in 1906. More relevant surely, her composer's ear could scarcely have forgotten the shimmering sonority of the weeping flowers, similarly scored, in *Where Do the Stars Come From?*, composed in 1902.

---

[96] The Glinka State Consortium of Musical Culture has since been re-named the Russian National Museum of Music.

Then came three contrasting discoveries. The first was the full orchestral score of the Piano Concerto, op. 2 in A Minor (1900) – not the published score but a manuscript in immaculately neat hand-writing, in ink, which had clearly been used at the premieres in Moscow and St Petersburg. Second was confirmation at last of Kashperova's residential address in Moscow, a detail that had for so long eluded my investigation. It was situated, by extraordinary coincidence, directly above my regular 'haunt', the café opposite the Conservatoire. However, nothing was to compare in terms of surprise and musical significance with the third discovery, File 345/4, the contents of which revealed the manuscript of a major *previously unknown* composition, a four-movement Piano Trio in A Minor. It was almost complete, clearly unperformed, and was very probably Kashperova's final composition. The work was premiered in Cardiff, after a two-year process of editing, on 18 December 2020 by the Gould Piano Trio as part of a concert on BBC Radio 3 broadcast to listeners across the United Kingdom and abroad, also heard in Russia.[97] With the restoration of this four-movement, thirty-five minute chamber work, Kashperova's catalogue and her musical reputation were both greatly enhanced for, to date, all her other large-scale mature compositions remain 'lost'. The search will continue, of course.

In her memoirs, Kashperova expresses the view that, notwithstanding the achievement of the Symphony, her Trio of 1912 (for viola, violoncello and piano) was 'the best thing I have ever written, but it was lost without trace, and I cannot rewrite it'. She clearly laments that the score of this precious achievement had not survived the tsunami of historic events. Yet, it is possible that the very act of committing this expression of regret to paper may have spurred Kashperova into creative action: to reverse Fate's injustice by composing another piano trio even though in Moscow there was no interest in her music at all, and no hope of a performance. In such circumstances it is clear that she now composed for her personal satisfaction alone, and for posterity.

This posthumous Piano Trio in A Minor reveals many subtle refinements to Kashperova's earlier musical idiom, the opening *Allegro agitato* and the *Finale* strikingly so. Harmonically, these movements can resemble some wild modulatory roller-coaster, twisting and turning, lurching even, from one key centre to the next, lending the music's otherwise lyrical rhetoric an unsettling unpredictability. There are structural innovations, too: neither the first movement nor the Scherzo conform to their customary sectional repeats. In this way, the musical drama is liberated from formal constraints, which are replaced by a

---

[97] BBC Radio 3 also broadcast the Gould Piano Trio's performance at the 2021 Edinburgh International Festival. See also www.boosey.com/cr/news/Kashperova-s-Piano-Trio-receives-broadcast-premiere/101689.

captivating sense of narrative, fluidity and impetus. Interestingly, Kashperova's mature piano writing is more conciliatory than it was in her youth when the brilliant Conservatoire graduate had been keen to demonstrate her prowess as Rubinstein's prize-winning student.[98] Rather, in this late trio, Kashperova blends the three performers into a wholly collaborative fusion. This is heard to particularly beautiful effect in the Scherzo, and in the *Andante*, which is beguiling in the extreme though never sentimental – a remarkable achievement given the circumstances of the work's composition.

Kashperova claimed, reasonably enough, that she could not re-write her beloved Piano Trio (with viola) of 1912, yet did she recall nothing? Might there be melodies or rhythms in the later Trio (in the identical key of A minor) which are, in some form, quotations or references? While the earlier work remains lost it is impossible to know for certain. Nevertheless, within the texture of her last sketches – which, due to the impossibility of performance, must have acquired in the composer's imagination the character of autobiographical writing, of a private 'confessional' – Kashperova has indeed woven a quotation from an earlier work. It is a short motif first heard in Romance no. 11 of *Songs of Love* (1904) 'Night Prayer' (Ночная молитва; Nachtgebet) – also in A minor. Could this be merely a coincidence? The frequency of this motif's appearance in both works suggests otherwise. The texture of the Trio's first and last movement, for example, is dominated by this four-note pattern. It is heard most clearly in the dynamic opening theme of the *Finale*, as B-A-C-B in bar 1. Indeed, it reappears throughout the movement, eventually leading to the work's energetic and emphatic conclusion.[99] In the song 'Night Prayer', the same motif features throughout, though subtly at first, in the accompaniment. In the opening bars this four-note pattern is delineated by the piano (as A-G#-B-A in bar 1; B-A#-C-B in bar 2) within the right-hand triplets – half-concealed, yet still audible and in its effect, off the beat, unsettling. There is a contrasting central section after which the opening material returns (at bar 63) though with a striking difference: the motif is transformed from background (keyboard) *accompaniment* into foreground (vocal) *melody*. It is a dramatic transformation to A major. Yet in a Schubertian sense, the major key only heightens the sense of pathos and anxiety. The soprano now sings the expressive four-note phrase constantly (b. 67: bb. 78–96) until the very end of the song, repeating her urgent, at times desperate appeal for divine assistance:

---

[98] Cf. Cello Sonatas, op. 1 and the Piano Concerto.

[99] Kashperova would have been well aware of the similarity of this pattern to J. S. Bach's musical cypher Bb-A-C-B natural, used to delineate B-A-C-H using German notation. Similarly, Kashperova's pattern is a melodic shape formed by intervallic relationships that can be transposed to any pitch.

How painful it is to say:
Our dream is at an end.
We are all exhausted
By life's unremitting struggle.
Lord have mercy!
Let our dreams sustain us
And renew our strength.
Lord have mercy!
Shield our mortal sins
With thy boundless Love.
Let us sleep in peace
And give us dreams of gold
During our nights of despair![100]

For composers of musical and intellectual stature nothing is written into the score by chance – the very thought is absurd. One must therefore consider Kashperova's inclusion of such a reference in her late Piano Trio as fully intentional. But why would she indulge in this sleight-of-hand? In the spirit of further enquiry, we might more closely investigate the song's *lyrics* and recall that Kashperova herself was the author of this intense poetry that the Piano Trio now summons directly from 'Night Prayer'. Poet and composer cry out with one voice: 'Lord, have mercy! / Renew our strength / Let us sleep in peace / And give us dreams of gold / During our nights of despair!'. If we seek a meaning for Kashperova's deliberately-coded 'message' we are surely drawn to understand her act of self-quotation *also* as an act of solidarity with her persecuted *tovarishchi* ('comrades'). By this, I am referring to those individuals of the musical, artistic and literary communities who were so severely treated during the Purges of the 1930s. By extension, of course, Kashperova may also have been referring to her fellow citizens – men, women and children, representatives of Russian society in general, including her own family – united in 'life's unremitting struggle'.[101]

One senses that Kashperova's appeal to the Almighty harbours nostalgia not only for Bochatino's irreplaceable idyll but also for her homeland's lost inno- cence. Kashperova left no written programme note or explanation. Of course not. Nevertheless, if such a reading reflects even a shadow of her conscious or subconscious intentions, then the Piano Trio in A Minor, penned during the 1930s (that notorious decade), represents much more than an artfully crafted demonstration of her musical talents. It stands as a monument to her ingenuity

---

[100] Translation: Patricia Cockrell. Kashperova, *Songs of Love: 12 Romances* (London: Boosey & Hawkes, 2022).

[101] This emotive appeal is reminiscent of the flowers' cry-for-help in *Where Do the Stars Come From?* (1902). In Polonsky's verses, translated as: *On earth a scene of dreams / And yet it seems / A starless sky, no stars at all / Where, O where is light? / No trace of stars, no moon, / No sign of love, no stars above.*

and inner strength in the face of unspeakable adversity, and to her courage and compassion expressed through her music. A piano trio like no other, it is a defiant and profoundly philosophical statement.

Kashperova, as we know, felt a particular affinity with chamber music, in her *Memoirs* recalling with pride the performance of her early Piano Trio in D at the Aeolian Hall in London. It is fitting, therefore, that her last composition should also be in this, her favourite genre. The Piano Trio in A Minor (*op. posth.*) is now published – an initiative authorised and encouraged by the Russian National Museum of Music, whose director, Mikhail Bryzgalov, and head of the manuscripts department, Dr Olga Kuzina, kindly granted me access to Archive no. 345 and permission to restore this and other Kashperova manuscripts. I shall be eternally grateful for the trust they showed in this English musicologist's abilities, respect-fully and accurately, to give voice to this veritable treasure of Russian culture.

At the time of writing, the Kashperova Edition is being launched by Boosey & Hawkes to coincide with International Women's Day 2022, exactly four years after the modern-day premiere of the Symphony in B Minor. I can only express my deepest appreciation to all those who have made the Kashperova Edition – and this Element – come to life. Neither would have been possible without the generous collaboration of musicologists, musicians, archivists, librarians, trans-lators and editors in both Russia and the United Kingdom.[102] All have shared a common sense of idealism and a determination to do what is right for Kashperova, whose name and whose beautiful compositions were forgotten so unjustly and for so long. It has been my good fortune (my Destiny, some have said) to have been 'chosen' for the task of restoring Kashperova to her rightful place in history, with the primary aim of returning her music to the concert stage. Just as important for me is knowing that Leokadiya Alexandrovna is once again acknowledged and appreciated in her beloved Russia.

Whereas Kashperova's Symphony in B Minor ends in the major key, with a coda blazing with light and an overwhelming sense of optimism, the Piano Trio in A Minor finale persists resolutely with the minor mode to the bitter end. The work's alternating moods of tenderness and tension across its four movements made a strong impact at its first performance, broadcast on BBC Radio, particu-larly so on its audience in distant St Petersburg listening to Kashperova's voice for the first time. The following message – emailed to the author moments after the vigorous conclusion had sounded – was written by Dr Nataliya Braginskaya, the Conservatoire's academic director: 'It appears that Kashperova was a strong, unsentimental woman. Yet her music can also be so fragile, delicate, tremulous, poetic and womanly – in the best sense of this word. Above all, her

---

[102] See Acknowledgements

Figure 4 Kashperova wrote the caption to this photo: 'With the painter
Kurbatov drinking tea in the garden'.

Note the samovar on the table and, curiously, the large leaf on the composer's head
supposedly to shield her from the sun but also probably to amuse the photographer,
possibly her husband Sergei Andropov. Mikhail A. Kurbatov (1874–1959) specialised in
creating life-size, painted, plaster-cast sculptures. They were admired for their scientific
value as much as for their artistry. His sculpture *Tolstoy* (1913) was so realistic that
Tolstoy's daughter Maria Lvovna, upon seeing it, apparently lost the power of speech for
a while (was literally 'struck dumb') due to its impact. Kurbatov also recreated Lenin's
cerebellum and brain, with incision. His large-scale installation *Lenin in his Kremlin
study* (1925) was commissioned by the Marx-Engels-Lenin Institute where Sergei
Andropov held a senior position.

Image: *courtesy of the Russian National Museum of Music, with thanks to Mikhail Bryzgalov
and Olga Kuzina*

tender lyricism covers a deep and dramatic undertone.'[103] It is a sentiment
shared, I believe, by all those who have come to know this composer's music.
Leokadiya Kashperova died on 3 December 1940 in what circumstances we do
not yet know. Her husband Sergei Andropov, after completing a mathematical

---

[103] Email received 18 December 2020.

treatise concerning the 'expansion of large numbers', died in 1956.[104] Alexei Kashperov, musicologist and son of Elizaveta, spent his final years sorting and cataloguing archive 345 before his death in 1970.[105] None heard the Piano Trio performed. However, with the premiere on 18 December 2020 Kashperova's final and most powerful message, universal in its significance yet also intensely personal in its expression, has at last been delivered – to be shared in perpetuity with the musical world.

**

2 The *Memoirs* of Leokadiya Kashperova (1929)

The original text of Memoirs *has been translated by Patricia Cockrell, Russianist advisor to the Kashperova Edition for Boosey & Hawkes. The present author has contributed commentaries and further information via footnotes [and in square brackets] to clarify unfamiliar personnel and repertoire, or other references.*

Introduction
Graham Griffiths

In the late 1920s, perhaps from a position of isolation or vulnerability, Kashperova was moved to reflect on her childhood, upbringing, and early career. The result was her *Memoirs*,[106] completed in 1929, though they remained unpublished during her lifetime. They were eventually published in 1968, coinciding with the delivery of her surviving documents and manuscripts to the Glinka State Consortium of Musical Culture, Moscow, by her last known relative, the musicologist Alexei Kashperov. The *Memoirs* trace the first thirty-five years of Kashperova's life, from her childhood in the Russian interior in the 1870s to her greatest professional success in London in 1907. Her eventful, often dramatic narrative is recounted at all times with restraint, humility even, and with gracious acceptance. It is up to the reader to perceive what Kashperova herself truly felt or was disinclined to reveal.

Despite the nostalgia discernible between the lines, Kashperova expresses herself without any hint of sentimentality or excess. Details of her prodigious

---

[104] See: 'Andropov Sergei Vasilievich' at www.geni.com (accessed 1 May 2021).

[105] Alexei V. Kashperov (1902–70), pianist and 'Teoretik', was the editor of the impressively comprehensive *Letters: A. N. Skryabin* (Moscow: Muzyka, 1965/2003). While preparing a new edition of Kashperov's volume in 2002–3 the publisher Valentina Rubtsova was unable to trace any living descendants or relatives (conversation with the present author, October 2016). To Alexei Kashperov and F. S. Fesenkova, his archivist colleague, this volume is respectfully dedicated. See Acknowledgements.

[106] Translation: Patricia Cockrell, 2019. Original text: L. A. Kashperova, Воспоминания [*Vospominaniya*; 'Memoirs'], ed. N. G. Fesenkova, in Музыкальное наследство [*Muzikal'noye Nasledstvo*; 'Musical Legacy'], vol. 2 pt 2 (Moscow: Muzyka, 1968), pp. 135–45.

musical talents, apparent from the age of four, are recounted as matter-of-fact. Ordeals at the hands of her domineering teacher Mme Muromtseva, which must have prepared her well for her future studies with Rubinstein, are recounted with equanimity. Memories of youthful recitals – whether locally, in Kostroma, or under the spotlight of Moscow's musical elite – are described with an eye to explain rather than to impress, despite the fact that, for today's reader, her feats of repertoire are astonishing for someone so young.

Even in St Petersburg, Kashperova treats her achievements at the Conservatoire lightly, leaving room for more profound commentaries in the ensuing *Recollections of Anton Rubinstein* (See Section 3). Far from dwelling on her own successes, she prefers to express her admiration for those distinguished musicians who inspired her to compose and to perform to an ever greater standard. Despite her youth, it is clear that such as the leading players at the Maryinsky Theatre and the Conservatoire – Leopold Auer (conductor and violinist), Aleksandr Verzhbilovich (professor of cello) amongst them – were keen to form chamber music partnerships with her. Auer even attended her debut in London at the Aeolian Hall in June 1907, excitedly telegraphing colleagues in St Petersburg that 'the press has gone wild!'.[107]

There is a tradition in Russian literature for autobiographical writings oriented towards 'early years', for example Herzen's *Childhood, Youth and Exile* and Tolstoy's three volumes *Childhood, Boyhood* and *Youth*. Kashperova's *Memoirs* are no literary classic to be compared with these, but in the course of her narrative she can be seen to develop her writing skills to such a degree that she is able, in the ensuing formality of her essay concerning the teachings of the legendary Rubinstein, and despite its analytical intent, to express herself with economy, elegance, occasional wit ('Luckily I caught measles' is a typical gem) and clarity.

**

The Memoirs of Leokadiya A. Kashperova (1929)
(An autobiographical account of the years 1872–1907)

Translated by Patricia Cockrell

I'm looking down from my pram at the grass poking up through the snow – that's my first memory. We lived at the time near the town of Lyubim in Yaroslavl Region [the Kashperova family home was situated mid-way between two regional capitals, Yaroslavl and Kostroma]. We had an estate of 173 desiatins and a large house [in the hamlet of Bochatino] about fifty versts

---

[107] Auer taught regularly in London in the summers of 1907–11.

Figure 5 Leokadiya A. Kashperova (1872–1940) ca. 1890 as a student at St Petersburg Conservatoire in the Special Piano class of Anton Rubinstein.
Image: *courtesy of the Russian National Museum of Music, with thanks to Mikhail Bryzgalov and Olga Kuzina.*

from the town.[108] My childhood was easy, but we began lessons early as was usual amongst the gentry. We started with English and French. I never did study Russian but, whilst playing lotto with my Nanny I looked at the words under the pictures. I surprised my parents and friends by learning to read fluently at four. And I surprised them further by devising my own names for musical notes, since I didn't know the real names but was able to recognise them by ear. Later, when I had learnt to read music, guests would find it amusing to ask me to guess the

---

[108] A letter dated 2 August 1888 from Kashperova's mother, Maria Aleksandrovna, to the admissions office of the St Petersburg Conservatoire gives the following address: 'Kostromskaya guberniya [Kostroma region], Buiski uezd [Buiski parish], Bochatino mansion, on the river Volga' (Central State Historical Archive: Archive 361/Inventory 3/File 3051). Lyubim is situated approximately 100 km northeast of Yaroslavl, historic capital of the Golden Ring cities. Former Imperial Russian units of measurement: 1 desiatin = approximately. 1.1 hectare; 1 verst = approximately 1.1 km (0.6 mi).

notes, often of dissonant chords, from another room. It was hard to pull me away from the piano. My mother started to teach me when I was four; then a kind and pleasant teacher was employed, Zinaida Fedorovna Khomutova, a pupil of [Anton and Nikolai] Rubinstein's mother [Katherina Khristoforovna Rubinstein]. In our first lesson, she showed me the C major scale and in the second lesson, to her great astonishment, I played her all the major scales. Each scale was a revelation for me. I felt especial passion for G major, and this has stayed with me my entire life.

At that time, I was already able to play a transcription of Siébel's aria 'Faites-lui mes aveux' from [Act 3 of] Gounod's opera *Faust* [1859], plus another piece in the form of a sonatina. I was struck by the fact that in the exposition the dominant had the upper hand, and then in the development there was a conflict, after which the main pitch gained the upper hand again, and I calmed down. It was for this reason that I called the dominant pitch 'hateful' (by which I meant 'hostile') but I saw the sub-dominant as an 'embellishment' and came to love with a passion the series of sub-dominants and tonics.

I remember my older brother boasting that he knew more than me. 'But what you don't know,' I said to him, 'is why the B flat enhances the F'. 'Why?'. 'Because it is a fourth'. After that he fully accepted my theoretical knowledge and stopped boasting.

I started lessons with Maria Fedorovna Fewson when I was six, and I am very much indebted to her. Until that time the musical pieces heard at home were mainly gypsy songs and transcriptions from opera. She brought into our musical orbit Mozart's Symphonies in G Minor [no. 40, K.550] and D Major [no. 38, K.504 'Prague'], as well as Beethoven's Septet [in E-flat, op. 20, 1800] and his First, Second, Third and Fifth Symphonies. These were all played at a measured tempo, but I was soon able to fathom their beauty. I studied with Miss Fewson for three years and experienced my first success on stage during the last of these years.

In Kostroma, where we spent the winter months, there was a children's musical evening. The first movement of Haydn's *Toy Symphony* was played, and they planned to perform Chvatal's *Jolly Sleigh Ride* which proved to be too difficult even for the adults.[109] They let me have the music for three days, and on the second day Fewson and I played the piece together on the piano at the rehearsal. Everyone was astonished, and I was invited to perform in the evening. I played Pakher's *Le Ruisseau* brilliantly, and it was after this that they began to

---

[109] Franz Xaver Chvatal (1808–79), Bohemian pianist and teacher, later based in Magdeburg; composed piano Methods and recital pieces which Schumann described as 'Stübchenmusik' (parlour music), e.g. *Alpenklänge, Miniatur-Bilder für Klavier, Historische Notizkalender für Musiker und Musikfreunde* (1861).

call me a pianist.[110] Of course, this turned my head even though I was pathologically shy.

We had to move to Moscow for the sake of my brother's education. They wanted to enrol me at the Conservatoire, but Fate had something else in store. My mother met a woman of high status who scared her by telling her that female students are not allowed to sit down in the presence of the teachers: they have to stand for the sake of their deportment. Unfortunately, my mother believed this rubbish. I was supposed to study with N. S. Zverev [Nikolai Sergeyevich Zverev, 1832–93; teacher of Rakhmaninov, Skryabin and Alexander Siloti] and he had already agreed to this. From Zverev it might have been possible to move to the person who had recently become my ideal teacher [for composition], S. I. Taneyev [Sergei Ivanovich Taneyev, 1856–1915; Director of the Moscow Conservatoire, 1885–89]. But my mother, on the advice of the same woman, registered me at the N. A. Muromtseva Music School, saying that it would be socially advantageous. Finding myself in a theory class with a multitude of children, I didn't speak to anyone, and was frightened of Muromtseva herself, who alienated me with her mannerisms and her pretence at sincerity beneath a high-class tone.

N. A. Muromtseva [Nadezhda A. Muromtseva, 1848–1909], a pupil of [Nikolai] Rubinstein's, was a talented teacher who was able to inculcate a stage presence in her gifted pupils.[111] She organised musical evenings and inspired her pupils to study their pieces diligently and to practise their scales, studies and exercises, but because of these evenings our repertoire was rather limited. There were two or three such evenings over the winter and then an examination in the spring; that is to say, a musical morning in Count [Pyotr I.] Kapnist's reception room.[112] Our lessons were to prepare us for these performances.

I can still recall my first lessons with Muromtseva. She stood by the piano saying, 'Louder, my child, I can't hear anything, louder, Leokadiya!' Then she

---

[110] Josef Pacher (1818–71), *Le Ruisseau – Etude de salon*, op. 34. It is marked *Vivacissimo*. Kashperova was nine years old when she performed this work, rated as 'Advanced' by its publisher Universal Edition, Vienna.

[111] Tchaikovsky reviewed her performance of Liszt's Piano Concerto no. 2 in A Major (S.125) in the 14 March 1874 (O.S.) edition of the 'Russian Register' (Русские ведомости): 'Madame Muromtseva then played, with consummate artistry, [Liszt]'s brilliant, though rather empty piano concerto. She is one of the finest virtuosi we have ever heard in [Moscow]. In addition to a faultless technique, Madame Muromtseva has masses of taste and expressivity. It is said that [Anton Rubinstein], after hearing her play during the first rehearsal, went into raptures. I think that such praise must mean more to Madame Muromtseva than any favourable press review, and so I need not add anything else' (trans. Luis Sundkvist, 2009), http://en.tchaikovskyresearch.net/index .php?title=The_Second_and_Third_Weeks_of_the_Concert_Season&action=edit. (accessed 22 January 2021).

[112] Grandson of Vasily V. Kapnist (1758–1823), poet, playwright, critic of serfdom in Russia.

would crouch down, look down at my fingers and say, 'Lift your fingers higher. Your knuckles are sticking out. Everything should be in one line. Keep your hand high. Your hand must stay calm and still!' Such remarks were torture for me. My thick short fingers refused to rise, my hand stayed hard as a piece of wood, and the more I played the harder my hand grew, and the more rigid my fingers became.

Later Muromtseva gave me a better suggestion as to how to gain strength. She gave me Prudant's fantasy *The Puritans*, directing my attention to the way the melodies sang.[113] This fantasy was an arrangement of an aria from Bellini's '*I Puritani*'. She explained the need to develop the singing quality of the piece with the help of the strength of one's fingers; that is by continuing to press down on the key after playing the note. She ended by saying, 'So you see how you have made this piece sing, or at least tried to. You need to practise all your scales and studies and learn all your pieces properly.' At the same time she would talk about the diligence of several female pianists, in particular Anna Melig, who used to play in her attic all day long, causing the ivory of the white keys to wear through to the wood. And when Sophie Menter's teacher Liszt once told her he wanted to play a duet with her, she practised fourteen hours a day and wore out the skin on her fingers to the extent of drawing blood.[114] She would soak them in vinegar to stop the bleeding and carry on playing despite the pain. I found confirmation of this in a German book, and as far as the ivory of the white keys is concerned, this was confirmed during one of the classes when Bulatova's ancient piano was used, the piano that she had played to death and replaced. I saw with my own eyes that the ivory, whilst not worn down completely to the wood, had become so thin that the wood beneath could be seen, and dark stains had formed. Muromtseva told me that Nikolai Rubinstein recommended that the entire room where you practise should be furnished with soft material to reduce the sound and develop strength.

Later, when I heard Anton Rubinstein and saw his hands like two globes, I wondered why I should keep my fingers in a straight and even line, when a globe can only be formed in a convex position. And why I had to keep calm hands high, holding the fingers rigid when it was necessary whilst playing to keep the hands loose in the form of a sphere? And why [I was told] to lift my fingers high

---

[113] Emile Prudant, French pianist (1817–63), briefly a pupil of Sigismund Thalberg, and composer of 'fantasies' on operatic themes (e.g. *Lucia di Lammamoor*, *I Puritani*) and *études* based on the music of other composers (e.g. *Souvenir de Beethoven, Souvenir de Schubert*).

[114] Sophie Menter (1846–1918), pupil of Franz Liszt (nicknamed *L'incarnation de Liszt*). Her playing was described by George Bernard Shaw, who heard her in 1890, as creating 'an effect of magnificence which leaves Paderewski far behind'. Quoted in Julie Ann Sadie and Rhian Samuel (eds.), *The Norton/Grove Dictionary of Women Composers* (New York: W. W. Norton & Company, 1995), p. 326.

and to achieve strength by pressing down on the key when, as Breithaupt says, you need the weight of your whole arm from the shoulder? **[1]**.[115] But I only started wondering about this much later and, in the meantime, I tried in vain to do as I was asked. Mama said, 'There'll soon be an evening recital and you'll be asked only to listen and that's how it will be until you learn to keep your fingers in the right position.' So, I carried on trying, even though it was difficult.

At my first recital there I gave a very successful performance of Kuhlau's *Sonatina* [Friedrich Kuhlau, 1786–1832] and Moscheles's *Polonaise*, opus 53 [Ignaz Moscheles, 1794–1870]. I can remember the occasion: as I entered, I saw lots of pupils but none of my group from the theory class. They didn't deign to come.

That year, Anton Rubinstein came to Moscow and gave several concerts. Muromtseva decided to bring three young female pupils to see him: one very young, one adult and her pride, Bulatova. I was the young pupil. The only comment Rubinstein made about me was that I sat too far back on the piano stool. As he left the room he said gently, 'Goodbye, my dear. Make sure you sit properly!' He kissed Bulatova on the head but said about Bach's second fugue that she had just played: 'It all depends on the way you see it.' So Muromtseva asked, 'How do you play it?' 'Quite differently: everyone plays this fugue *staccato,* but I play it *legato.*' Later I was able to hear how magically Rubinstein played this *legato*; the fugue acquired a serious, elegiac character rather than the gavotte that one usually hears. **[2]**

That was the year I had to play Mozart's Third Concerto at an evening performance, and for the exam I played the third movement of Kalkbrenner's Concerto in D Minor [no. 1, op. 61].[116] For the first time in my life somebody chose to print a review about my performance: 'The still young Miss Kashperova demonstrated great talent in her playing. The long third movement of Kalkbrenner's Concerto was played with lightness and depth. We can expect a great deal of her when she matures.'

I played Bach's *Allemande* and *Bourrée* plus Liszt's Fantasy on *'Lucia'* [*Réminiscences (Marche et Cavatine) de Lucia di Lammermoor,* 1836] at the first musical evening of the following year. I also played both these pieces for Rubinstein and earned the following remark: 'She has a good resonant tone'. Rubinstein said something else complimentary, but I can't remember what it

---

[115] Numbered notes in square brackets, **[1]**, **[2]**, etc., refer to the original notes in the first publication of *Memoirs* (Moscow, 1968), which can be found at the end of this section. Rudolf Breithaupt, 1873-1945, author of *Die natürliche Klaviertechnik*, 1905, and *Die Grundlagen der Klaviertechnik,* 1906.

[116] Friedrich Kalkbrenner, 1785–1849, German pianist and composer, based in Paris: dedicatee of Chopin's Piano Concerto no.1 in E Minor, op. 11 (1830).

was, and he said that I must work on the trills. Bulatova also earned his approval, but Monigetti had an attack of nerves and didn't play at her best.

Many things happened that year. Firstly, I joined the harmony class of V. P. Prokunin [Vasily P. Prokunin, 1849–1910; composer, pianist, folklorist], a wonderful teacher who praised me and said that I should take special lessons. I started taking interesting lessons with him and these went on for two years, during which time I managed to cope with strict counterpoint and composed some complicated pieces for five and six voices, but I hadn't yet written any complete fugues. In any event, Lyadov, with whom I had also been studying for a short while, asked me to write a chorale with figured bass in a free style, and he was pleased with the result, saying, 'Yes, you've captured it.' I know that I am wholly obliged to V. P. Prokunin for this because my professor at the conservatory, N. F. Solovyov [Nikolai Feopemptovich Solovyov, 1846–1916], reacted negatively to counterpoint: 'For Kashperova this is poison.'[117]

The other great events at this time were the Historical Concerts given by Anton Rubinstein. It is impossible to recall these without rapture. Rubinstein, pianist, musician and man, appeared in all his glory creating an overwhelming impression. Immature as I was, I still realised that all the great composers were being paraded before me in a magnificent panorama. Of course, Beethoven was the highest placed, and of all his compositions, the *Appassionata,* and the Theme and Variations [the final movement] from his Sonata opus 109 were at the top of the list. The theme from this piece once woke me up at night. I clearly heard an authentic human voice penetrate my soul, and this voice brought me to tears.[118]

The symphonic concerts under the direction of Max [von] Erdmansdörfer [1848–1905] were also major events for me. I had started to go to symphony concerts and was lucky to be able to experience the emotion and life that such a talented conductor brought to his performances.

To give her students the chance to experience chamber music, Muromtseva invited the violinist A. Kolakovsky [Alexei Kolakovsky, 1856–1912, pupil, with Jascha Heifetz, of Leopold Auer][119] to join our classes. I played all the sonatas of Mozart and Beethoven with him including the Kreutzer Sonata,

---

[117] See '1912' under Section 1. Kashperova is complemented for the 'impressive contrapuntal effects' in her Piano Trio.

[118] The theme is marked: *Gesangvoll, mit innigster Empfindung. Andante molto cantabile ed espressivo.*

[119] The Hungarian violinist Leopold Auer, 1858–1930 followed in Wieniawski's steps as the foremost violinist in St Petersburg where he was based for forty-nine years and was much admired by Tchaikovsky. Among his most famous pupils was Jascha Heifetz. Auer performed in London in a piano trio with Anton Rubinstein and Alfredo Piatti. He was later to perform chamber music with Kashperova and Aleksandr Verzhbilovich.

which I performed at one of the recital evenings. It was at this time that I was overcome with the urge to struggle with difficult pieces: I played Beethoven's *Appassionata*, the Kreutzer Sonata [op. 47 in A major] and Liszt's *Lucretia Borgia* [*Réminiscences de 'Lucia Borgia' de Donizetti*] and also his twelfth Rhapsody [*Hungarian Rhapsody,* no. 12, in C# minor]. In the first year of my studying with her, Muromtseva had said to me, 'You will turn all heads with your talent. You have a lot of strength, perhaps too much, but this strength is not used wisely.' This was true; I applied strength of will to everything, playing all the pieces not just at a satisfactory level but well. With my temperament I could distract listeners from noticing my lack of technique. This I was to acquire later.

A. A. Kolakovsky, a pupil of Auer's, was a brilliant violinist, strong and deep with a large tone and sensitive expression. As one of those who did not notice my faults, he constantly praised me. I learnt everything for him with a passion so that Muromtseva expressed displeasure, saying that I have become careless as a soloist and was playing only for the violin. But it wasn't so. I was the one who had asked her if I could play the *Appassionata* and I played it with such passion that I had great success at one of the recital evenings. But this [being a solo pianist] wasn't enough for me – I wanted to play chamber music too.

One of my acquaintances in Kostroma organised a charity concert at which I was to be the leading musician. The programme, which my mother had put together, comprised a Mozart fantasy, a Chopin study, Thalberg's fantasy *Don Juan* [Sigismund Thalberg, 1812–71, *Serenade and Minuet from* Don Giovanni], a Field Nocturne,[120] Mendelsohn's *Song of the Spinning Wheel*, the *Wedding March* and the *Dance of the Elves* from the music to *A Midsummer Night's Dream* by Mendelsohn, transcribed by Liszt, a Song without Words by Mendelssohn, a Bourrée by Bach, the Twelfth Rhapsody by Liszt, and the *Russkaya and Trepak* by Anton Rubinstein [op. 82, no. 6]. I played all this with strength and brilliance. It was a great success.

The four of us spent New Year's Eve in a railway carriage [most probably, en route to visit relatives]. Father counted up to twelve, and we wrote down our wishes and burnt them. 'What shall I write?' I asked my mother. 'Write: to study under Rubinstein,' she said. So, that's what I wrote.[121] My parents decided at this time to move to Petersburg for my sake. We were all hoping I could become

---

[120] John Field, b. Dublin 1782, lived in Russia from ca. 1820 and died in Moscow in 1837. His piano Nocturnes caught the interest of Chopin for their 'vague aeolian harmonies, these half-formed sighs floating through the air, softly lamenting and dissolved in delicious melancholy'. From Liszt's preface to his edition of Field's *Nocturnes* (1859).

[121] At New Year, at the first chime of the midnight bells it is a Russian tradition to write one's wish on a tiny scrap of paper, then quickly burn it, shake the ashes into a glass – champagne for adults, something suitable for children – and drink it all up before by the final, twelfth bell for good luck.

a pupil of Rubinstein's, but when Mama and I went to discuss this with him he refused outright, even though he was pleased with my performance of the first movement of Beethoven's Sonata no. 7 [in D, op. 10, no. 3] and Kullak's octave study [Theodor Kullak, 1818–82, *School of Octave Studies*, op. 10, no. 3 in D]. While I was playing, a woman with a clever and pleasant face, though not beautiful, sat next to Rubinstein. He turned to her for advice about my studies. We went through to the next room, and on our way out the woman advised me to study with Professor Chezi, if he would agree. But he was ill, so Mama and I had to return to Moscow.

I decided to study on my own that summer. To register for class five, I had to reach a certain standard in science subjects. Mama had a painting teacher, a charming German woman who had spent the previous summer with us and who was planning to come again this year. She recommended her nephew, the son of a pastor, and he prepared me so well that I passed the exams. He made a deep impression on me. We corresponded for several years and then lost touch.[122]

I was in Petersburg again in the autumn where I took an exam in the theory of composition, in which I wanted to specialise, on the advice of Prokunin. The person who examined me was a younger man, prematurely grey, short and with beautiful dark eyes. This was A. K. Lyadov [Anatoly K. Lyadov, 1855–1914]. I got to know him later. I played the Scherzo of my composition (in D major of course) [title unknown] and sang the entire sol-fa immaculately, but, as Lyadov told me later, in a horribly shrill and childish voice. The examiner said, 'This is truly a genuine student.'

The exams in general subjects took place the following day. Russian language was first. I had spent all summer writing explanations and comments on sayings or proverbs, as demanded by the programme for entering class five, but by mistake the teacher set me an essay analysing [Gogol's] *The Government Inspector*.[123] Of course, I didn't dare say that I am taking the entrance exam for class five, not six. In tears I managed to write about ten or fifteen lines. The teacher said, 'That will have to do.'

The other exams went well, and I was admitted to class five. It could be that the teacher of Russian realised he had made a mistake, but I was sad that I hadn't shone with the analysis of sayings and proverbs that I had worked on all summer.

The piano exam took place the following day. They kept me waiting from 10 a.m. until 5 in the evening I was the last to be called. I summoned my courage

---

[122] Correspondence written on floral notepaper, from Kashperova to Pastor Heinrich Adolf Gillot of the Dutch Reformed Church on Nevsky Prospect, is held at the Central State Historical Archive of St Petersburg: archive 2110/ inventory 1/file 222.

[123] Satirical play written in 1836 by Nikolai Gogol (1809–52).

and played Bach's fugue well, and Liszt's fantasy on *Les Huguenots* [by Giacomo Meyerbeer, 1791–1884], which I had prepared myself, brilliantly with all the strength of my temperament. The effect was stunning, and it was here that the woman who had heard me play before, in the spring, began to play a role in my life. She was Sofia Alexandrovna Malozyomova [1845–1908, a former student of Anton Rubinstein], a teacher and later professor at the Conservatoire.[124] She began to persuade Anton Grigorievich to take me on, and several other professors joined in. Anton Grigorievich said, 'I will accept her, but she will join Solovyov's composition class, as it is not acceptable to have two specialities.'

I had my first lesson with Rubinstein the next day. A lot of the people who habitually come to observe his lessons had gathered in his room. He sat at one grand piano, his pupils at another. When he wasn't satisfied with a phrase, he played it tirelessly several times over. It was a great joy to learn straight from the hands of a genius and to try to express the same mood and feelings that he wanted, and in the way that he wanted. His main demand was that one should experience the piece of music intensely and be able to express this experience. Here my instinctive playing was inappropriate; it was essential to think in order to grasp what I was being taught, to listen carefully, and to adapt my customary rigid and stressful technique. I found this very difficult. For the most part we played Bach's preludes and fugues, and Beethoven's sonatas. I worked well on Bach and on Beethoven's Third Sonata [in C, op. 2, no. 3], and also on the *Pastoral* Sonata [no. 15 op. 28] and [no. 18] opus 31 no. 3. Rubinstein then gave me Schubert's *Moments Musicaux* [D.780], which I managed well, though I found these more challenging. Beethoven's Sonata [no. 27] opus 90 was less successful: I couldn't capture the drama of the first movement, and the only way that I could manage the left-hand tenths was to play them as arpeggios. He got angry and said, 'You are only pretending to have small hands.' I found this offensive and hurtful. Besides, I was worn out after the first months of stressful piano studies, special harmony lessons and general studies. Luckily, I caught measles and after this Rubinstein forgot about the unsuccessful sonata and gave me Schumann's *Fantasiestücke* [op. 12], which went well. He was especially pleased with the second piece *Aufschwung*, which suited my temperament.

The special harmony lessons involved attending lectures by professors and composing various works including chorales and preludes and modulating

---

[124] S. A. Malozyomova (1845–1908), pianist and teacher, studied under Leschetizky and Rubinstein at the St Petersburg Conservatoire. Previously she had attended the Smolny Institute (1863–66), the college 'for Noble Maidens' founded by Catherine the Great. Kashperova was accepted as a piano teacher at the Smolny Institute in the spring of 1916 but resigned in the autumn of that year (see Section 1).

preludes, which I found easy thanks to the technique of voice-leading that I had learnt from V. P. Prokunin.

My first year at the Conservatoire went well. Under Solovyov I transferred to the counterpoint class, which he hated, considering it poison for me.[125] Along with this he started to give us short pieces [to compose]: Minuets, Songs without Words, Scherzos and Waltzes. I wrote these brilliantly. Solovyov was very pleased and showed my pieces to Rubinstein who said, 'She will eclipse all the men at the Conservatoire, but not all the men in the world.' Anton Grigorievich was also pleased with my piano studies. I began to play more complicated pieces: Bach's *Chromatic Fantasy and Fugue* [BWV 903], Schumann's *Kreisleriana*, Beethoven's Sonata [no. 21] opus 53 ['Waldstein'], and as before, we continued to play Bach's preludes and fugues from the *Well-Tempered Clavier*.

There were four of us [in Rubinstein's 'elite class' – see Figure 6]. A fifth pupil had been dismissed from the class the previous year because Anton Grigorievich was not satisfied with him. Two of the most able were graduating this year. One of them, [Yevgeny] Holliday [1871, St Petersburg – ?], who had an English father and Russian mother, had a beautiful virtuoso talent, which, combined with the firm musical foundation he had received from Anton Grigorievich, made him an outstanding pianist. The other, [Sofia] Poznanskaya [1870 Vilna – 1947 Warsaw], a special favourite of Rubinstein's, had a singing, bewitching tone, great strength and brilliant technique. Holliday chose to play Liszt's Concerto in E flat, and Poznanskaya chose Rubinstein's Concerto [no. 4] in D minor. Anton Grigorievich appointed [Sophie] Yakimovskaya (1873 – ?) to accompany Holliday, and me to accompany Poznanskaya. The composer's presence really scared me, but I managed to accomplish my task so well that Auer called me 'Kapellmeister'. Thus ended my second year at the Conservatoire.

Holliday and Poznanskaya gave their debut concerts the following year, each performing a different concerto. Yakimovskaya and I continued our studies with Anton Grigorievich.

Knowing that Rubinstein was planning to leave the Conservatoire and move to Dresden, Yakimovskaya decided to bring forward her graduation despite the wishes of Anton Grigorievich. I accompanied her [performance of] Beethoven's Fourth Piano Concerto. I could not consider accelerating my studies too, as I was the younger pupil and had only been at the Conservatoire for three years. It was decided that I would graduate in two years' time, as an external student. Anton Grigorievich set up a separate exam for me in his office, and so many people came that there was standing room only. I played the fugue from Bach's Partita in B Minor, Mozart's Fantasy in C Minor, and Beethoven's *'Lebe Wohl'* Sonata [op. 26, 'Das Lebewohl'],

---

[125] See Section 1 (n. 26) for a witness statement by S. Maikapar.

Последние ученики
А. Г. Рубинштейна

153

Figure 6 'The Last Pupils of A. G. Rubinstein', ca. 1890: Standing, left to right: Leokadiya Kashperova, Eugene Holliday. Seated, left to right: Sophie Yakimovskaya, Sofia Poznanskaya.

Image published in Anton G. Rubinstein, Музыка и ее Представители: разговорь о музыке [*Music and Its Representatives: A Musical Conversation*], 3rd ed. (St Petersburg: Artists Union Press, 2005 [1891]).

Schumann's *Faschingschwank* [*aus Wien*], the Nocturne in F minor and the Polonaise by Chopin, and Liszt's *Somnambula* [Fantaisie sur des motifs de l'opéra *La Sonnambula* de Bellini, S.393]. He was very pleased.

It would seem that I should study really seriously the following year since Anton Grigorievich had promised to come for ten days in January and he wanted to hear me play, but I made some mistakes. Firstly, having learnt Anton

Grigorievich's Sonata, the third one [in F, op. 41], and having played it well at
S. A. Malozyomova's musical evening, I played to Anton Grigorievich not
this but Chopin's Fourth Ballade [in F minor, op. 52] which I hadn't learnt
properly, because without his lessons I lacked stimulus. I also played for him,
but not well, Schumann's Sonata in F Minor [no. 3, op. 14]. I had somehow
lost my way and began to work carelessly. This was a lost year for my piano
studies. A high point of the year for me was playing Beethoven's Piano Trios
in D major [op. 70, no. 1, 'Ghost'] and Bb major [op. 97, 'Archduke'] and
Schumann's D minor Trio [op. 63] with F. N. Hildebrandt and his brother
[violinist and cellist]. I worked on these pieces with great pleasure.
Hildebrandt was very pleased with me, and he introduced me to [the cellist,
Aleksandr] Verzhbilovich [1850–1911: professor of cello], whose admirer I
had been for a long time. Having heard Hildebrandt praise me, Verzhbilovich
asked me what we could play together. Deeply embarrassed, I said nothing.
My friend came to my rescue by naming a trio, but Verzhbilovich said this is
played too much and suggested a different one. I thought he was joking. I can't
express how happy this great artist's musicianship made me at public and
private concerts. I am boundlessly grateful for the warmth and the care he
showed me right up to his death. I keep these memories shining in my soul. I
expressed my sense of gratitude towards Verzhbilovich in the two sonatas I
dedicated to him [Cello Sonatas, op.1, no. 1 in G Major and no. 2 in E Minor].
I also dedicated to his memory the Trio for piano, viola [*sic*] and cello, the best
thing I have ever written, but it was lost without trace, and I cannot rewrite it. I
should have written a new one.

The year is 1893, I was planning the repertoire of my graduation pro-
gramme: Rubinstein's Fantasy Concerto in C Major [Fantasy for Piano and
Orchestra, op. 84], Bach's Toccata in C Minor [BWV. 911], Mozart's
Variations from his D Major Sonata [K.576], Beethoven's Trio in E-flat
Major [Piano Trio, op. 70, no. 2], Schumann's Sonata in G Minor [no. 2, op.
22], an impromptu by Chopin and Liszt's *Pest Carnival* [*Hungarian
Rhapsody*, no. 9 in E-flat, 'Carnival in Pest']. It all went beautifully, and the
concerto accompanied by Felix M. Blumenfeld [composer, 1863–1931] was
so brilliant that it was decided to overlook the fact that I was only considered
to be a pupil of the Conservatoire in the theory of composition.[126] I was
awarded First Prize – a Schröder grand piano.[127] I appeared in the programme
as a former student of A. G. Rubinstein. I think my guardian angel S. A.
Malozyomova had organised this. A telegram was sent to A. G. Rubinstein

---

[126] For piano she was *externom* – an external pupil.
[127] C. M. Schröder was a leading manufacturer of grand pianos based in St Petersburg. A family
business since 1818, the firm was nationalised by the new Communist state in 1918.

from the director, Y. I. Johanssen and from professors Bernhardt, Lavrov, Lyadov, Tolstoy, Punch and Malozyomova: 'Kashperova. Famoser Kerl. Nie dagewesener Erfolg' ['Kashperova. Famous fellow. Unprecedented success'].

I was supposed to be preparing for my own concert and for performing with a symphony orchestra, perhaps with this same C major Fantasy of Anton Grigorievich's, but instead I spent the remaining days visiting friends before going [home] to the country.[3] My first duty was to visit my dear friend Sonya Poznanskaya, who was expecting her first child. She was very pleased for me. She herself had been awarded not only a Schröder grand piano but also a Becker grand, which the firm [J. Becker – manufacturer of Tchaikovsky's piano][128] had given in that jubilee year for the best pupil. I was very pleased to accept the congratulations of my friends and acquaintances. At last Mama and I set off for the country.

I enjoyed myself all summer without thinking about preparing a concert programme, and when I was invited to play with a quartet,[4] I played in such a way as to have good memories of this. Everyone advised me to present my own recital, but I had no programme prepared, and I had no time to think about this: I was still living on the memory of the quartet concert when I had enjoyed for the first time the beautiful sounds of Verzhbilovich's cello. [Leopold] Auer of course was also magnificent [1845–1930: professor of violin], but I felt some sort of special link and affinity with Verzhbilovich. He probably felt this too because he invited me to take part in his recital. But here – alas! – I was out of luck. At first, he opted to play a Boccherini sonata then, ten days before the concert, he changed this to the Chopin Sonata [in G Minor, op. 65, 1845] thinking that I probably knew it already. But I had never seen this sonata. If I had not been so shy, I would have admitted this and asked for at least two rehearsals. But, trusting in me, he completely forgot about me, and the rehearsal, the only one, took place on the day of the concert. Of course, I was very anxious and unsure and so I played nervously and too forcefully and was criticised in a newspaper article, and more worryingly by Auer. But a favourable review in another newspaper consoled me. However, Verzhbilovich did not abandon me: he soon invited me to perform with him again and with Hildebrandt at a friend's house, and then at another house. From that time onwards, I joined his circle of friends and started to visit him and his wife, a very pleasant and kind woman.

This friendship could not have failed to leave an impression on me: I had graduated [1895] from the composition class at the Conservatoire

---

[128] Jacques Becker – 'Facteur de pianos. Maison de la Comtesse Tolstoi à St.-Pétersbourg' – was founded in 1841. It merged with Schröder in 1903. All Russian Empire piano manufacturers were united in 1924 to produce one Soviet model named *Red Oktober*.

(not brilliantly with a 5, but only with a 4.5), and my first independent composition was a Sonata for piano and cello [Cello Sonata, op. 1, no. 1 in G], dedicated of course to Verzhbilovich. I wrote it in the summer and wanted to show it to him in the autumn but changed my mind. Later I timidly admitted that I had written a Sonata for piano and cello. When we had played the first movement he exclaimed, 'What a surprising lady you are! How beautiful this is, and how it suits the cello!' We continued with the Scherzo, then the elegiac and melodic *Andante*, which he played excellently, and then the rather immature and naïve Finale, after which we fell into each other's arms. I was ecstatic. But it didn't end there: Verzhbilovich played my Sonata at a concert organised by the Music Society for a certain singer, and then he played it at his own recital. He also showed it to Rimsky-Korsakov and to Lyadov. Both were pleased with the composition, but Lyadov pointed out some places that showed technical and compositional immaturity, especially in the *Andante*, where he suggested changing the middle section. He offered a few lessons to help with this. But my friends did not like this new version, so I published the Sonata without the changes. I soon wrote a second Cello Sonata, which was also published. It was performed at the Kerzins' concert series in Moscow and by the quartet in Petersburg, where Verzhbilovich played it beautifully.[5]

For these first attempts at composition and for the acclaimed *Russian Serenade* for cello [*Русская серенада*, 1908], which he played in public more than once, I am indebted to Verzhbilovich. In spite of their faults, Verzhbilovich and many other cellists liked them for their freshness. Later compositions, the twelve romances [*Songs of Love: 12 Romances*] and the Trio for piano, violin and cello [Piano Trio in D, op. 3], were also noted for being fresh and sincere. The Piano Concerto and the Symphony were, in my opinion, weightier, and I feel that the Trio I wrote for piano, viola and cello [1911; 'lost without trace'], dedicated to the memory of Verzhbilovich, had some good qualities.[129]

Returning to my piano performances I remember especially playing Rubinstein's Fifth Piano Concerto [in E-flat, op. 94] with a symphony orchestra, and my own Piano Concerto [Piano Concerto, op. 2 in A Minor, 1900], which I played in Moscow and in Berlin. My Symphony [Symphony, op. 4 in B Minor, 1905] was also played in Berlin, thanks to my patrons. There were some positive notices and there were some bad ones, but I was well received by the public.

---

[129] Also described as 'The best thing I have ever written.' The review in the *Russian Musical Gazette* noted 'although the mood is gloomy and mournful the music is not sentimental, no sweet sighs or nostalgia. Instead, the score conveys a strong and convincing individuality. Of particular note are the two final movements (out of four): the Scherzo and the Theme & Variations are written with an excellent sense of sonority between the instruments and with some impressive contrapuntal effects.' See '1912' under Section 1.

But my main success abroad was in the summer [of 1907] in London [i.e. a greater success, in Kashperova's opinion, than the performances of her Symphony and Piano Concerto in Berlin. She valued it so highly perhaps because in London she performed her Piano Trio – a clear demonstration of the elevated value she assigned to chamber music]. I played with great joy, and the notices were all good. Auer, who came to my concert, wrote [in a telegram sent to St Petersburg], 'All the newspapers have gone wild.'[130] **[6]**

Such concerts were financially supported by piano pupil friends who became my patrons. I had to give a lot of music lessons, because after the death of my father [1898] and the illness of my brother our material circumstances were poor. It was only possible to build a concert career by appearing abroad, but this demanded a good deal of time and money. Even Poznanskaya, who had tried to perform abroad, ended up by getting married; Yakimovskaya too.[131] After my trips abroad I could no longer ask for help from my friends. It would have been possible to take up teaching activities at the Conservatoire where the most gifted students gather, but the director [Julius] I. Johansen [grandfather of Leopold van der Pals, 1884–1966, composer-in-residence at Rudolf Steiner's Goetheanum at Dornach, 1935–66] dissuaded me from this. He suggested, as did [Auguste] R. Bernhard [Glazunov's predecessor as Director of the Conservatoire], one of the examiners at the time who was well disposed towards me, that it might be better to start in a private school. Bernhard told me bluntly, 'They'll eat you up at the Conservatoire.' So I accepted the offer from the director of the Petersburg Music School [Josef] A. Borovka to teach in his school and I started work, as always, with passion but with no particular plan: I tried to encourage my pupils to study music in its broadest possible sense, as they didn't seem properly prepared for their performances. But the director was my good friend [See '1919' in Section 1] and the pupils were very fond of me, and when my sister [Elizaveta, dedicatee of *In the Midst of Nature*] started at this school and became the centre of my class as a consequence of her charming character, the atmosphere brightened even more. But my sister got married, and I left the school to everyone's regret after working there for ten years [1897–1907]. This coincided with my trips abroad and I needed to be totally free for these.

---

[130] Auer had performed a series of concerts in London in 1868, including Beethoven's *Archduke* Trio with Anton Rubinstein and Alfredo Piatti. He travelled to London in 1905 to coach the fourteen-year-old Mischa Elmann before his London debut in Glazunov's Violin Concerto in A Minor, op.82 – a work dedicated to Auer. He regularly taught in London in the summers of 1907–11.

[131] See Section 1 (n. 48) for information about the distinguished career of Sofia Poznanskaya in Poland. See also Figure 6.

Rejoicing at my successes but not having built a career, I threw myself
headlong into the family lives of my sisters, in their joys and sorrows, continuing in the winter to give private lessons and concert appearances. And on
Tuesdays I had musical evenings at home. My life was completely full.

**

Notes by F. S. Fesenkova 'with the assistance of J. I. Milstein' (Moscow, 1968):

1. For further information about Breithaupt see website: www.cambridgeurl
   .com – Notes by F. S. Fesenkova to 'Recollections of Anton Rubinstein',
   Note **[10]**.

2. The second fugue (C minor) from Book 1 of *Das Wohltemperierte Klavier*
   by J. S. Bach, like almost all the other fugues [in this work] has no indica-
   tions in the manuscript score regarding [its] interpretation.

   In the 1830s the first annotated edition to be published was edited by Carl
   Czerny [1791–1857], who pointed to the necessity of performing this C minor
   fugue *staccato*. In the 1883 edition (Leipzig: Steingräber) Hans Bischoff [1852–
   89] suggested that this fugue should be played *legato*. Undoubtedly, Anton G
   Rubinstein knew both editions, but one cannot say that he borrowed his [*legato*]
   interpretation from Bischoff. Rubinstein was an artist of such genius that he was
   able to [arrive at the decision to] play *legato* utterly independently of the
   Bischoff edition.

3. L. A. Kashperova performed Rubinstein's Piano Concerto no. 5, op. 94 in Eb
   major in St Petersburg at the 10th Symphonic meeting of the Russian Musical
   Society under the direction of Max Erdmansdörfer on 23 December 1895.

4. On 28 November 1895, L. A. Kashperova participated in the 5th Quartet
   meeting of the branch of the Russian Musical Society. She performed
   Rubinstein's Piano Quartet op. 66 in C Major with L. S. Auer [violin], F.
   N. Hildebrandt [viola] and A. V. Verzhbilovich [violoncello]. [This work is
   dedicated to Pauline Viardot-Garcia and was completed following
   Rubinstein's meeting with Turgenev in Paris in 1863.]

5. The second Cello Sonata of L. A. Kashperova, op. 1, no. 2 in E minor, was
   performed in Moscow on 16 January 1911 at the 102nd concert of the Circle
   of Russian Music-Lovers by A. S. Luboschutz [Ana Luboschutz, 1887–
   1975, Gold Medal-winner, Moscow Conservatoire, 1908; the first Soviet
   cellist to be awarded the title 'Honoured Artist of the U.S.S.R.'] and
   [Victoria] Miller-Khoroshevsakaya [pf.].

6. L. S. Auer often visited London. Apparently, the meeting with Auer mentioned by Kashperova took place in 1905 when he arrived in London in connection with the debut of his student Mischa Elman [Fesenkova is under a misunderstanding – see p. 55 for clarification of the date].

3 *Recollections of Anton Rubinstein* (1929) by Leokadiya Kashperova

Translated by Roger Cockrell
Full text available via the Element website:
www.cambridge.org/Graham_Online appendix

Introduction

Graham Griffiths

Kashperova's *Recollections of Anton Rubinstein* offer an instructive and fascinating exposé of her experiences as a student of the legendary pianist Anton Rubinstein (1829–1894).[132] Initially Kashperova offers an expansive introduction to her theme. In the second part, the musical examples with commentary provide a detailed description, down to the weight and phrasing of a single note, of how Rubinstein performed and taught specific works. The *Recollections* are vivid and informative in equal measure, in a manner rarely, if ever, portrayed in previously available literature about Rubinstein. Thanks to Kashperova's evident concern to pass on her experience for the benefit of others, her recollections also contain advice of practical relevance, even, for today's pianists – especially those embarking upon a professional career.

When Kashperova and three other specially selected pianists studied with Anton Rubinstein, between 1888 and 1891, he was in his very final affiliation to the St Petersburg Conservatoire, shortly before his death. His lessons ran for four hours on Wednesday and Saturday afternoons and were open to other students from within the Conservatoire. The observers would crowd into the room and down the corridor, just to be present and to glean what they could from 'the heart and soul of St Petersburg', the very founder of the Conservatoire, Russia's internationally acclaimed pianist-conductor-composer. While they could only observe this star at a distance, Kashperova circulated in his inner orbit for four intense years 'feeling the heat', as it were, of Russian music's most celebrated son – and most respected father figure.

Rubinstein's unhurried gait, his stern no-nonsense expression, his Beethovenian head and shock of leonine hair – all combined to create an impressive and

---

[132] Translation: Roger Cockrell, January 2019. Original text: Kashperova, *Vospominaniya*, pp. 145–68. The original title is *Recollections of A. G. Rubinstein*.

imposing appearance, leading Kashperova, in one of her many mots justes, to reflect that Rubinstein had been 'carved out of a single piece of granite'. And how he used his lion's roar, which Kashperova describes as 'the thunder in his voice', to communicate his most heartfelt, inspirational invective! 'You are playing a Sonata by Beethoven! Down on your knees!' On other occasions, his response could be merely offhand. When asked about fingering he would reply: 'Play it with your nose if you like. I don't care!' Such an apparently disengaged attitude belied his extreme sense of responsibility to his students. In 1889, Kashperova recalls, even in the thick of an intense schedule of rehearsals and concerts organised to celebrate his sixtieth birthday he was 'astonishingly conscientious, never missing a single class'. Certainly, purely technical matters did not concern him. 'I don't give lessons,' he would say, 'I give advice' – or insight, according to Alexander McArthur, the Irish pianist who travelled twice to St Petersburg to observe Rubinstein's teaching. He writes that Rubinstein's lessons 'are studies in poetry, in insight, in the conception of the ideal of the great masters, rather than lessons in the ordinary sense'.[133]

Kashperova's account is unparalleled in Rubinstein literature for its sympathetic yet frank testimony, for its musical and technical detail, and for the precision of its references to specific details in repertoire by Bach, Schubert, Beethoven and Liszt. Furthermore, Kashperova displays keen awareness of pianistic traditions, both historical (Czerny, Chopin and Liszt) and contemporary (Alexander Siloti, Moriz Rosenthal and Josef Hoffmann) comparing them objectively with Rubinstein's approach and her own. In the process, she draws of Rubinstein a finely etched and sympathetic portrait that does much to contradict the generally accepted, censorious view that this titanic pianist endorsed a less-than respectful treatment of other composers' wishes, particularly with regard to tempo. Rather, Kashperova describes how Rubinstein sought to instil in his students 'such a chaste attitude towards performing' based (1) on their acknowledgement of the supreme authority of the composer, and (2) insisting that they respect every last detail in the score, *especially* with regard to dynamics and tempo.

Rubinstein's one-liners have entered musical folk-lore. Kashperova recounts many gems here as they happened, in context. In the process, she reveals how these pearls of educational 'wisdom' – whether playful, domineering, amusing, cantankerous, teasing or downright offensive – were received at first hand, not as anecdotes, but by those directly impacted by such forceful remarks. Three of the quartet of students were female and on occasion Rubinstein could not resist teasing them with such taunts as: 'You're playing like a young Princess!' or,

---

[133] Alexander McArthur, *Anton Rubinstein: A Biographical Sketch* (Edinburgh: Adam & Charles Black, 1889), p. 112.

wearily, 'Les femmes, les femmes!' At other times he might step over the line: 'Keep all that energy for your husband when you get married!' While admitting that this 'reference to marriage was very offensive', it seems that such was his pupils' loyalty this would never develop into an issue: 'All the same, we could tell from his tone if he was angry or if it was simply a good-hearted joke.'

This side of Rubinstein's complex persona is familiar territory. More serious are charges of his supposed lack of artistic integrity, as reported by Josef Hofmann (1876–1957), that Rubinstein would actively encourage tampering with the score: 'Just play first exactly what is written. If you have done full justice to it and still feel like adding or changing anything, why, just do it.'[134] Yet, such reporting cannot be left un-contextualised. Is one to believe from this that he treated *all* composers equally in this fashion? Kashperova's closely observed account of the man and artist at work presents a completely different philosophy, one that adjusts the previous imbalance to suggest a far more selective approach. True, Rubinstein would grant himself liberties with tempo for expressive purposes in the music of Schubert, for example, but 'never with a note of Beethoven's music … since it was precisely this that exemplified his power and style'. His respect for Beethoven was unshakable. Far from harbouring a cavalier attitude to tempo, it was one of Rubinstein's main concerns, together with style. If his pupils' performance became too indulgent with either, he would rein them in with the caution: 'Le trop c'est l'ennemie du bien.' The pianist should always represent the composer's wishes responsibly by combining several factors, giving each careful consideration. These should include phrasing, tone, a sense of narrative, colour, character, drama, a sense of 'mystery' even or, when required, the employment of harsh sounds, which he also embraced: it was not always a case of 'keeping within the bounds of the beautiful'. All this, with due attention to tempo and rhythm, should be employed in the pianist's pursuit of style, forever the ultimate goal.

To illustrate Rubinstein's teaching, 'lovingly dwelling on every detail', Kashperova introduces twenty-six musical examples from Schubert (his *Moments Musicaux*) and Beethoven (his early- and middle-period sonatas, including *The Tempest* (op. 31, no. 2) and *Appassionata* (op. 57)). Thus the reader may more fully appreciate Rubinstein's subtler orientations representative of the more refined guidance he reserved for his most advanced pupils. Several subtleties of pianistic art are addressed: refinements such as tone colour, skills of phrasing, trills, the employment of the 'secret pedal', the proper use of the metronome, *Gewichtstechnik* and his own views regarding the position of

---

[134] Harold C. Schonberg, *The Great Pianists* (London: Victor Gollancz, 1964), pp. 355–6; quoted in John Rink (ed.), *Musical Performance* (Cambridge: Cambridge University Press, 2002), p. 333.

the arm and the shape of the hand and fingers. Rubinstein would demonstrate constantly throughout his four-hour lessons, evidently thrilling his pupils with his effortless display, for example, of triplets 'sounding like a ribbon'.

He would demand 'intense concentration and uninterrupted commitment to the spirit of the music' at all times. On the rare occasions when his students succeeded in this super-human task to his entire satisfaction he would shake them by the hand 'with such affection that it seemed to us as if the sun had just risen. And when he next met us, he would remember and start praising us again'.

Kashperova rounds off the *Recollections* with some wisdom of her own. Her advice may be appreciated even today by every aspirant pianist, for she shares her own experience generously and, in so doing, provides some valuable recommendations concerning the practical challenges of an emerging career. These include, *pace* A. G. R., finding the absolutely correct tempo for each piece, a notoriously difficult task, for which Kashperova comes up with a novel solution. She recommends that the pianist consider 'the principle contained in the Greek teaching of rhythm', which she explains as follows: 'With the Greeks, the fundamental unit of rhythm was not the longest note, as with us, but with the very shortest, consisting, when singing, of a single syllable. The Greek word for this is *mora*.' Applying this principle to Beethoven's Piano Sonata no. 1 in F Minor, she proposes that in the first movement the *mora* is 'clearly a quaver, in the second movement a semi-quaver, in the third a quaver again, and in the fourth a crotchet'.

In her closing remarks Kashperova again demonstrates her empathy with the young professional: 'Anyone who has performed in public will know how difficult it is,' she writes, 'how often it can go wrong – if, for example, the room is cold, or you feel under the weather, if there is an unresponsive audience.' Her advice involves a surprising combination of physiology and psychology: 'You will need to work very hard on the suppleness and sensitivity of your fingers, to prevent any such chance circumstances affecting [what she calls] *the current emanating from your emotions and your will-power and passing on down into your fingers.*'[135] Every effort must be made so as not to weaken this 'current' for the result will be a loss of rhythmic control – another of Rubinstein's great themes.

By reading *Recollections* one may even slip into Stravinsky's shoes and imagine the content, tone and direction of that two-year course of lessons with Kashperova between 1899 and 1901 that was of such benefit to him, as he would later (rather begrudgingly) admit.[136] If Rubinstein's dedication to the spirit of music knew no bounds, then his students' dedication to him was also

---

[135] Italics added.
[136] For a discussion of this topic, see Graham Griffiths (ed.) *Stravinsky in Context*, chapter 3: 'Leokadiya Kashperova and Stravinsky: The Making of a Concert Pianist'.

limitless, appreciative of the priceless value of being guided by an artist of such stature: 'Everyone was aware of the significance of the occasion,' Kashperova writes with a mixture of reverence and self-deprecation. 'In his great kindness, this great musician has agreed to listen to us playing wrong notes and to correct our errors, sacrificing the best hours of his invaluable time for our sake.' Observer and Rubinstein biographer Alexander McArthur supports this view of his generosity: '[Rubinstein's] charity was unceasing. No-one gave more freely or more kindly or cared so little for the trouble he gave himself, provided he could do good.'[137] Not only pianists, but also scholars of Russian music history, of nineteenth-century pianism and of comparative teaching methodologies will gain much from *Recollections of Anton Rubinstein*, Kashperova's authentic, affectionate and revelatory witness account.

Recollections of Anton Rubinstein is available via the Element website:
www.cambridge.org/Graham_Online appendix

---

[137] Alexander McArthur, 'Rubinstein: The Man and the Music' – obituary article (1895), p. 32; see also, *Anton Rubinstein: A Biographical Sketch* (Edinburgh: Adam & Charles Black, 1889). See Bibliography and Further Reading.

Catalogue of Compositions

1. Compositions Published during Kashperova's Life – with Opus Numbers

Op. 1: Two Sonatas for piano and violoncello (1895–6). No. 1 in G Major; No. 2 in E Minor.

Op. 2: Piano Concerto in A Minor (1900).

Op. 3: **Trio in D Major** for violin, violoncello and piano (1904). Material not located.

Op. 4: **Symphony in B Minor** (1905). Orchestral score and an arrangement for piano solo made by the composer with the assistance of Balakirev (ca. 1909).

Op. 5: Unknown

Op. 6: Unknown

Op. 7. *Children's Tales in Song* (1907). Text: Maria Alexandrovna Kashperova.

> 'Shura is in the Village', 'The Little Foal', 'The Cat', 'Shura's Tantrums', 'The Billy-Goat', 'The Children', 'The Mother', 'The Herd Moves Along'.

** **

2. Published Compositions with No Opus Numbers

The Eagle and the Snake (1902). Ballade for baritone and piano. Text: Y. P. Polonsky.

To a Child in Answer to the Question: Where Do the Stars Come From? (1902). Legend for soprano, baritone, SSAA chorus and piano. Text: Y. P. Polonsky.

Songs of Love – 12 Romances for voice and piano (1902/1904). Text (Russian and German): L. A. Kashperova for voice and piano. Completed '12 January 1904'.

> Part 1 ('Dreams'): 'I Look Up', 'I Love You (1)', 'Prayer', 'Longing', 'Autumn Wind', 'I Love You (2)'.
> Part 2 ('Reality'): 'On my Way', 'Meeting', 'I Am Waiting for You', 'The First Frost', 'Night Prayer', 'In the Spring'.

In the Midst of Nature. Suite for piano solo (1910).

> 'Two Roses', 'Two Autumn Leaves', 'The Murmuring of the Rye', 'The Threshing of the Wheat'.

** **

3. Posthumous Compositions

Evening & Night for SSAA choir (n.d.). Text: Y. P. Polonsky.
Piano Trio in A Minor for violin, violoncello & piano (n.d.).

**

4. Assorted Unpublished/Incomplete Compositions (Russian National Museum of Music: Archive 345)

Choral/chamber works:

Белый слон ('The White Elephant') for choir and piano, [incomplete] (n.d.).
Над душистыми цветами ('Fragrant Flowers'), (n.d.).

Choral/a cappella works:

Правило Христовой веры ('The Rule of Christian Faith') for mixed choir [text unknown] (n.d.).

Chamber music:

Trio for Violin, Cello and Piano in Eb Minor [incomplete] (n.d.)

Piano solos:

Polonaise (1889)
March (1890)
Andante No. 1 in F Major (1890)
Allegretto (5 April 1892)
Andante Grazioso in C Major (1895)
Andante (Fugue) in A Minor (n.d.)
Andante (F Major); Allegro (C Major) (n.d.)
Allegro (n.d.)
Allegro (n.d.)
Valse (n.d.)
'Piano Selection': Scherzo (F major); Valse (D major); Scherzo (D minor); 'Chanson sans parolles [*sic*]', no. 1 (B major); 'Chanson sans parolles [*sic*]', no. 2 (B major); Valse (G major); Menuett [*sic*] (B minor) (n.d.)

Piano duets:

Duet (1887)
Duet: 'Le bateau à vapeur' (31 December 1887)
Duet: 'Petit Marche' (n.d.)

Songs, vc & pf

Беспорядки у феи ('Fairy Riots'). Text: Konstantin Balmont.

День рождения белки ('Squirrel's Birthday'). Text: Ivan Nikitin.

Утро ('Morning'). Text: Ivan Nikitin.

Песня о рекрутах ('A Song about Recruits'). Text: Sergei Esenin.

По селу тропинкой ('Taking the Path through the Village'). Text: Sergei Esenin.

Пред образом спасителя ('Before the Image of Our Saviour'). Text: Aleksei Koltsov.

Фейная война (*Fairy Warfare)* I. 'Fairy Riots' (Text: Konstantin Balmont); II. 'Across Dark Lawns' (Text: Ivan Vekhin); III. 'Light snow' (Text: Strakhova); IV. 'Father Frost's Secret' (Text: A. Krylov); V. 'The Chicken Run' (Text: Leokadiya Kashperova).

Цветы ('Flowers'). Text: Leonid Afanas'ev.

Six songs with lyrics by Leokadiya Kashperova:

Мальчик розу увидал ('A Boy Saw a Rose').

Если я умру на море ('If I Die at Sea').

Как на дубе на высоком ('On a Tall Oak').

К кончине Ленина ('Upon the Death of Lenin'). 'For the 9th Children's Colony of the Pushkin settlement' (1924).

Край ты мой заброшенный ('My Abandoned Land').

О, плачьте, печальные мои очи ('Oh, Weep, My Sad Eyes').

5. Lost Compositions (Not Located at the Time of publishing this Element)

Overture, for symphony orchestra (1894).

Orvasi, cantata for soloist(s), choir and orchestra. Text: D. S. Merezhkovsky (1895).

Paradise and the Peri, cantata. Text: Thomas Moore (n.d.).

Piano Trio in D, op. 3 (ca. 1906–7).

Russian Serenade, for violoncello and piano (1908).

Sonata for Piano & Violoncello no. 3 in F (1908).

Hommage aux œuvres de Pietro Canonica – seven piano solos (1912).

Incl.: *Armonia d'anima*; *Primavera*; *Aurora ridente* (other movements unknown).

Piano Trio for Viola, Violoncello and Piano (1912).

6. Writings

L. A. Kashperova, Воспоминания (Memoirs, 1929), ed. N. G. Fesenkova; Воспоминания об Антоне Григорьевиче Рубинштейне (Recollections of Anton Grigorievich Rubinstein, 1929), in Музыкальное наследство (Musical Legacy), vol. 2, pt 2 (Moscow: Muzyka, 1968), pp. 135–68.

7. Recordings (Welte-Mignon, ca. 1910. St Petersburg/Moscow).

Two recording sessions:

a) **Balakirev**: Toccata in C# Minor (piano roll no. 2034); Valse no. 6 in F# Minor (no. 2035); *Gondola Song* (2036); [2037]; **Kashperova,** *In the Midst of Nature* (no. 2038); **Cui**, Prelude, op. 16, no. 15, in Db (no. 2039).

b) **Balakirev**: Sonata no. 2 in B Minor, Mov. 1 (no. 2162); Mov. 2 (no. 2163); Mov. 3 (no. 2164). Available on YouTube: www.youtube.com/watch?v=ePaWef3WYdQ&t=67s

Further information:

www.boosey.com/composer/Leokadiya+Kashperova

Bibliography and Further Reading

Reference

Boosey & Hawkes, 'Kashperova Edition' (2022), www.boosey.com/composer/Leokadiya+Kashperova.

Cohen, Aaron I. (ed.), *International Encyclopedia of Women Composers*, 2nd ed., revised and enlarged (New York: Books & Music USA Inc., 1987).

Hoffmann, Freia, 'Kaschperowa, Kašperova, Kashperov(a), Kaschperow, Kaschpérow, (Elikonida) Leokadia, Leocadi, Léocadie, Aleksandrowna, verh. Kaschperowa-Andropowa', Europaïsche Instrumentalistinnen-Lexikon, Sophie Drinker Institute (2018), www.sophie-drinker-institut.de/kaschperowa-leokadia.

Kashperova, Leokadiya A., Воспоминания [*Memoirs*], ed. N. G. Fesenkova, in Музыкальное наследство [*Musical Legacy*], vol. 2, pt 2, (Moscow: Muzyka, 1968), p. 135.

Sadie, Julie Ann and Rhian Samuel (eds.), *The Norton/Grove Dictionary of Women Composers* (New York: W. W. Norton & Company, 1995).

Энциклопедии, Словари, Справочники, *Entsiklopedii, Slovari, Spravochniki*. Y. V. Keldish (ed.) (Moscow: Izdatel'stvo 'Sovetskaya Entsiklopediya', 1974).

Archives

Central State Historical Archive of St Petersburg. Archive 2, Inventory 1, File 18996; Archive 7, Inventory 2, File 1793.

The Musical Museum, Brentford (London): Welte-Mignon piano rolls.

Russian National Library, St Petersburg; Fontanka Music Library; Manuscripts Department/Balakirev Archive; Kashperova materials.

Russian National Museum of Music (Glinka Consortium of Musical Culture), Moscow. Archive 345.

Journals/Music Review Sections

Mährisches Tagblatt (St Petersburg), 20 November 1895.

The Sunday Times (London), 23 June 1907.

The Times (London), 7 October / 23 October 1907.

Musikalischen Wochenblatts (Leipzig), 17 October 1907.

The Musical Standard (London), 2 November 1907.

The Violin Times (London), December 1907.

Langrish, Kate and Graham Griffiths, 'Forgotten Female Composers', Programme book, LSO St Luke's (London), 8 March 2018.

Walter, Viktor, 'A *Clavierabend* with L. A. Kashperova', *Russian Musical Gazette*, vol. 16 (1912).

Online Resources

'Andropov, Sergei Vasilievich', Geni, www.geni.com.

Arts & Humanities Research Council, 'Forgotten Women: International Women's Day in Russia 1917', (interview with Graham Griffiths; 8 March 2017), www.ahrc.ac.uk/research/readwatchlisten/features/kashperova.

Di Laccio, Gabriella (ed.), DONNE – Women in Music, www.facebook.com/donneuk.

Griffiths, Graham, 'Getting to Know Leokadiya Kashperova', Drama Musica, YouTube video (8 June 2018), www.youtube.com/watch?v=eLmN_Y62c-g.

Griffiths, Graham, 'Dr Graham Griffiths in Search of Leokadiya Kashperova', Drama Musica, YouTube video (8 June 2018), www.youtube.com/watch?v=iOVjjrAnhDg.

Grover, Ed, 'Forgotten Composer's Symphony Performed for First Time in 100 Years Thanks to City Researcher': www.city.ac.uk/news/2018/march/leokadiya-kashperova-bbc-radio-3-forgotten-female-composers.

Books and Articles

Bernhardt, G. B. and I. M. Yampolsky, *Кто писпл о музыке* [*Who Wrote about Music*] (Leningrad: All Union Publishers Sovetskiy Kompozitor, 1974).

Braginskaya, Natalia (ed.), *Nikolai Andreyevich Rimsky-Korsakov (1844–1908): The St Petersburg Conservatory – Documents and Materials*, vol. 3 (St Petersburg: Blagovest, 2019).

Cui, César. A., *Избранные письма* [*Selected Letters*], ed. I. L. Gusin (Leningrad: State Music Publishers, 1955).

Cui, César. A., *Избранные статьи об исполнителях* [*Selected Concert Reviews*] (Moscow: State Music Publishers, 1957).

Droucker, Sandra, *Erinnerungen an Anton Rubinstein: Bemerkungen, Andeutungen and Besprechungen in seinen Klassen in St-Petersburger Konservatorium* [*Memories of Anton Rubinstein: Observations, Recommendations and Reviews of His Teaching at the St Petersburg Conservatoire*] (Leipzig: B. Senff, 1904).

Dyachkova, L. S. and Boris Yarustovsky (eds.), *I. F. Stravinskiy: stat'i i material'I* [*I. F. Stravinsky: Articles and Documents*] (Moscow: Sovetskiy Kompozitor, 1973).

Griffiths, Graham, 'Leokadiya Kashperova and Stravinsky: the Making of a Concert Pianist', in Graham Griffiths (ed.), *Stravinsky in Context* (Cambridge: Cambridge University Press, 2021), pp. 24–33

Griffiths, Graham, *Stravinsky's Piano: Genesis of a Musical Language* (Cambridge: Cambridge University Press, 2013).

Horgan, Paul, *Encounters with Stravinsky* (Middletown: Wesleyan University Press, 1989).

Hunnius, Monika, *Mein Weg zur Kunst* [*My Path to Art*] (Hamburg: Verlag tradition-GmbH, 1925).

Korabelnikova, Ludmila, *Alexander Tcherepnin: The Saga of a Russian Emigré Composer* (Bloomington: Indiana University Press, 2008).

Kuzina, Olga, 'Unknown Tchaikovsky manuscripts in the Odoyevsky Archive', in *Almanac*, no. 2, ed. M. P. Rakhmanova (Moscow: Glinka State Consortium of Musical Culture, 2003).

McArthur, Alexander, *Anton Rubinstein: A Biographical Sketch* (Edinburgh: Adam & Charles Black, 1889).

McArthur, Alexander, *Rubinstein: The Man and the Music* (n.p., 1895).

Novikov, V. I., *Ленин и деятельность искровских групп в России (1900–1903)* [*Lenin and the Activities of the Iskra Groups in Russia (1900–1903)*] (Moscow: Thought Press, 1984).

Rittermann, Janet, 'On Teaching Performance' in John Rink (ed.), *Musical Performance* (Cambridge: Cambridge University Press, 2002), pp. 75–88.

Rubinstein, Anton G., *Музыка и ее представатели: Разговорь о музыке* [*Music and Its Representatives: A Musical Conversation*] (St Petersburg: Artists Union Press, 2005 [1891]).

Schonberg, Harold C., *The Great Pianists* (London: Victor Gollancz, 1964).

Stravinsky, Igor, *An Autobiography (1903–1934)* (London: Marion Boyars, 1990).

Stravinsky, Igor and Robert Craft, *Memories and Commentaries* (London: Faber and Faber, 2002 [1960]).

Taruskin, Richard, *Stravinsky and the Russian Traditions. A Biography of the Works Through* Mavra, vol. 1 (Oxford: Oxford University Press, 1996).

Varunts, Viktor, *I. F. Stravinsky: Perepiska s russkimi korrespondentami – Materialy k biographii* [*I. F. Stravinsky: Russian Correspondence – Documents and Biographies*], vol. 1 (Moscow: Sovetskiy Kompozitor, 1988 [1977])

Walsh, Stephen, *Stravinsky: A Creative Spring: Russia and France 1882–1934* (London: Pimlico, 2002).

Zaytseva, Tatyana A. (ed.), *Наше святое ремесло: памяти В.В. Нильсена, 1910–98* [*Our Hallowed Craft: A Memorial to V. V. Nilsen, 1910–98*] (St Petersburg: Sudarynia Press, 2004).

Acknowledgements

Dr Rhiannon Mathias, Bangor University.

Dr Katharina Brett, Cambridge University Press.

Patricia Cockrell and Dr Roger Cockrell, translators of 'Memoirs' and 'Recollections of A. G. Rubinstein'.

Dr Kadja Groenke, Luisa Klaus and Freia Hoffmann, Sophie Drinker Institute, Bremen

Dr Natalia Braginskaya, editor-in-chief *Opera Musicologica* (St Petersburg Conservatoire)

Lyudmila Yaroslavovna Milchakova, 'N. A. Rimsky-Korsakov' Conservatoire of St Petersburg

Natalia Mikhailovna Gubina-Shepherd, Exeter–Yaroslavl Twinning Association, Exeter House, Yaroslavl.

Dr P. John Shepherd, University of Exeter.

John Minch, James Eggleston, Jeremy Allen, David Allenby, Brontë Larsen-Disney, Emma Kerr, Boosey & Hawkes (London).

Tetyana Ursulova-Rosenfeld: New Bodleian Library, University of Oxford.

Tatiana Danilovna Rebrova.

Nicola Oatham and members of the Oatham-Edwards and Griffiths families.

**

St Petersburg: Elena Nekrasova; Larisa Miller; Tatiana Zaytseva; Maria Lyudko, soprano; Maria Sergeeva and librarians (St Petersburg Conservatoire); Lidia Ader (Rimsky-Korsakov Museum-Apartment); Irina Bezuglova, Sofia Pepelzhi (Russian National Library, Fontanka); Oxana Shevchenko, pf. and Christoph Croisé, vcl. (Berlin); Andrey Rumyantsev and Irina Borisovna Sheluchina (Central State Historical Archive of St Petersburg); Galina Kopitova (Institute of Fine Arts); Olga Manulkina (Smolny Institute, St Petersburg University); Nataliya Mansour (European University of St Petersburg); Lyubov Osinkina. **Moscow**: Mikhail Bryzgalov, Olga Kuzina and Elena Fetisova (Russian National Museum of Music); Irina Torilova, head librarian, 'Irina 2' (Moscow Conservatoire); Librarians of the Lenin (Music) Library; Mark Zilberquit, Anna Razinkova and

Valentina Rubsteva (Muzyka/Jurgensen Music Publishers); Alyona Rostovskaya, soprano. **Moscow and Venice**: The F. I. Stravinsky Family Fund; Anastasia Kozachenko-Stravinskaya; Igor Kozachenko and Evgeniya Dobrotina; Yuri Dobrotin and Lisa McGarva. **Rostov-on-Don**: The librarians of the Rostov-on-Don Conservatoire. **Yaroslavl**: Murad Annamamedov, conductor (Yaroslavl Academic Governor's Symphony Orchestra); Irina Ginsburg; Natalia Borisova, conductor (Renaissance Choir); Ensemble Barroko; Nataliya Khryashcheva (Mayor's Office: Department of Foreign Affairs); Alla Khatyshkhina (Arts Museum); Marina Polyvranaya; T. P. Senchugova; Alla Anosovskaya (Sobinov Museum); Svetlana Shubina (Sobinov Music College); Irina Ivanovna Zenkina; the librarians of the Yaroslavl District Library, music division. **Kostroma**: Nina Fedorovna Basova (Kostroma Regional Library); Lyubov N. Semenova; Larisa Pukhacheva. **Lyubim**: Viktor Gurin (Lyubim Historical Museum). **Magdeburg**: Anna Skryleva, conductor (Magdeburg Philharmonic Orchestra). **Amsterdam**: Guillermo Brachetta. **Terraube**: Susan Edward, vlc; David Levi, pf. **City, University of London**: Miguel Meira; Stephen Cottrell; Lauda Nooshin; Ian Pace; Anna Tremain; Ed Grover. **Guildhall School of Music and Drama**: Laura Roberts, pf; Yoanna Prodanova, vlc. **University of Oxford**: Jonathan Cross. **University of Sheffield**: Mary Sackett. **BBC**: Luke Whitlock (Radio 3); Peter Thresh (New Generation Artists); Neil Varley (BBC Concert Orchestra); Jane Glover, conductor; BBC Singers; Hilary Campbell, conductor. **New Generation Artists**: Menjie Han, pf; Andrei Ioniță, vcl; Lilit Gregorian, pf; Anastasia Kobekina, vlc; (Luka Okros, pf.) **Abingdon**: Kurt Rosenfeld. **Ardingly**: Curtis Schwartz (Curtis Schwartz Studio). **Brighton**: Debbie Venn. **Chichester**: Susie Duffin (West Sussex Record Office). **Danehill**: Christian Heinrich; Matt Mockridge; Glen Rowlan; Pascale Williams, Patrick Wigan (Cumnor House School). **London**: Gabriella di Laccio (DONNE: Women in Music); The Gould Piano Trio (Lucy Gould, Richard Lester, Benjamin Frith); Alexander Karpeyev, pf (Pushkin House); Ann Sheffield, vlc; Naoko Sonoda, pf; Maria Zachariadou, vlc; Richard Leach, pf; Benjamin Ely (Player Piano Group); Julian Dyer (Julian Dyer Piano Rolls); Rex Lawson and Denis Hall (The Pianola Institute); William 'Bill' Webb, conductor. **Reading** (Arts & Humanities Research Council): Sarah Burgess. **Steyning**: Jacquie Burgiss, Janet Pennington (Steyning Museum). **Uckfield**: David Newbery; Barbara Darlington; Robbie Cannon (Quarry Print).

10 April 2014

St Petersburg Conservatoire: Music Library.

11.35 a.m.

Q: Извините, у вас есть партитуры Леокадии Кашперовой?

('Excuse me, do you have any scores by Leokadiya Kashperova?')

A: Кто? (Who?)

11.38 a.m.

Symphony in B Minor (1905) by Leokadiya Kashperova is located.

Note (Figure 7) the composer's hand-written dedication to Glazunov, newly appointed Director of the Conservatoire: 'To the most highly-esteemed Aleksandr Konstantinovich, with respect and gratitude from the author'. Kashperova later adapted the work for piano solo, a copy of which is in Balakirev's library held at the Russian National Library annex, Fontanka, St Petersburg. Symphony in B Minor was performed on International Women's Day, 8 March 2018, by the BBC Concert Orchestra, conductor Jane Glover, at LSO St Luke's, London, and broadcast live on BBC Radio 3, with the collaboration of Boosey & Hawkes (London) and the Arts & Humanities Research Council (United Kingdom).

**

Figure 7: The front cover of Kashperova's Symphony in B Minor (St Petersburg: V. Bessel', 1905) held in the Library of the St Petersburg Conservatoire.
Image: *courtesy of the 'N. A. Rimsky-Korsakov' St Petersburg Conservatoire.*

To Alexei Kashperov (1902–70)

Musicologist, who donated L. A. Kashperova's materials to the Glinka State Consortium of Musical Culture (since renamed the Russian National Museum of Music).

To N. S. Fesenkova.

Archivist (Russian National Museum of Music, Moscow),

who edited Memoirs *and* Recollections of A. G. Rubinstein *for publication in 1968; and catalogued the Kashperova Archive (no. 345), 1968–71.*

Cambridge Elements ≡

Elements in Women in Music

Rhiannon Mathias
Bangor University

Dr. Rhiannon Mathias is Lecturer and Music Fellow in the School of Music and Media at Bangor University. She is the author of a number of women in music publications, including Lutyens, Maconchy, Williams and Twentieth-Century British Music: A Blest Trio of Sirens (2012), and gives frequent conference presentations, public lectures and radio broadcasts on the topic. She is also the editor of the Routledge Handbook on Women's Work in Music (forthcoming), a publication which arose from the First International Conference on Women's Work in Music (Bangor University, 2017), which she instigated and directed. The success of the first conference led to her directing a second conference in 2019.

About the series

Elements in Women in Music provides an exciting and timely resource for an area of music scholarship which is undergoing rapid growth. The subject of music, women and culture is widely researched in the academy, and has also recently become the focus of much public debate in mainstream media.

This international series will bring together many different strands of research on women in classical and popular music. Envisaged as a multimedia digital 'stage' for showcasing new perspectives and writing of the highest quality, the series will make full use of online materials such as music sound links, audio and/or film materials (e.g. performances, interviews – with permission), podcasts and discussion forums relevant to chosen themes.

The series will appeal primarily to music students and scholars, but will also be of interest to music practitioners, industry professionals, educators and the general public.

Cambridge Elements ⹀

Elements in Women in Music

Elements in the series

Grażyna Bacewicz, the First Lady of Polish Music
Diana Ambache

*Leokadiya Kashperova: Biography, 'Memoirs' and 'Recollections of
Anton Rubinstein'*
Graham Griffiths

A full series listing is available at: www.cambridge.org/ewim

Printed in the United States
by Baker & Taylor Publisher Services